"This book provides important information for a new HR professional. Many of the questions regarding the interviewing process are also vital to those who are looking for positions."

> — Gloria Pincu, President,
> Basic Learning Systems, Inc.,
> Asheville, NC
> Gloria@basic-learning.com

"The book has more than 365 answers, it is quite comprehensive, from A to Z. It is evident that it is well-researched since it targets the details an entrepreneur needs to have a solid HR foundation and manage the staff while complying with federal and state regulations. It should be on the shelf within arm's reach of the owner or HR Manager."

> — David H. Arechiga,
> DHA Associates, since 1988
> *Human Resources Consultants,*
> *HR solutions*
> dha5@hotmail.com
> Ret. Administrator,
> Human Resources at Columbia
> University

"This book is great for the small business owner who wears many hats, one being that of the HR Director. You will get the information you need to manage your personnel issues successfully, without the added expense of a HR person. Well worth the investment."

— Ken Patterson Sr.
ASM/EMT/PSM/CSSO
kensr@aug.com

"As an entrepreneur who has started several successful businesses over the years, I have dealt with hiring, firing, and all of the personnel management work that goes in between that tries to compensate, motivate, protect, and control my employees. With the laws constantly changing, I never knew the latest rules, and I learned through trial and error. This book would have saved me many sleepless nights, stressful meetings with tearful employees, and trips to my lawyer's office. Why learn from my own mistakes when I could have learned from the experts through this book? I would rather refocus all of that wasted time and energy on growing my business. For me, the decision is clear - buy this book!"

— Kevin Aguanno
Executive Project Manager, IBM

365 Answers About Human Resources for the Small Business Owner

What Every Manager Needs to Know About Workplace Law

by Mary B. Holihan

365 Answers About Human Resources for the Small Business
Owner: What Every Manager Needs to Know About Workplace Law

Copyright © 2006 by Atlantic Publishing Group, Inc.
1210 SW 23rd Place • Ocala, Florida 34474 • 800-814-1132 • 352-622-5836–Fax
Web site: www.atlantic-pub.com • E-mail: sales@atlantic-pub.com • SAN Number: 268-1250

ISBN-13: 978-0-910627-78-8
ISBN-10: 0-910627-78-9

Library of Congress Cataloging-in-Publication Data

Holihan, Mary B., 1947-
   365 Answers About Human Resources for the Small Business Owner: What
Every Manager Needs to Know About Work Place Law / Mary B. Holihan.
   p. cm.
   Includes bibliographical references and index.
   ISBN 0-910627-78-9 (978-0-910627-78-8)
1. Small business--Personnel Management. 2. Labor Laws and Legislation.
3. Personnel Management. I. Title. II. Title: Three Hundred and Sixty-Five
Answers About Human Resources for the Small Business Owner.

   HF5549.H5237 2006
   658.3--dc22   2006012536

EDITOR: Paula Casteel Angermeier
PROOFREADER: Jackie Ness • jackie_ness@charter.net
GLOSSARY: Christina Mohammed
COVER DESIGN: Studio 6 Sense • info@6sense.net • www.6sense.net
ART DIRECTION & INTERIOR DESIGN: Meg Buchner • megadesn@mchsi.com
BOOK PRODUCTION DESIGN: Laura Siitari • www.siitaribydesign.com
Printed in the United States

Table of Contents

Chapter Five
Interviewing Candidates   81

Chapter Six
The Hiring Process   95

Chapter Seven
Orientation, Training and Career Development 111

Chapter Eight
Communicating with Employees   133

Chapter Nine
Evaluating and Motivating Performance   145

Chapter Ten
Discrimination and Fair Treatment   159

Chapter Eleven
Establishing Compensation Plans   177

Chapter Sixteen
Labor Relations and Collective Bargaining 241

Chapter Seventeen
Performance Problems, Discipline Procedures, and Termination 251

Conclusion 263

Resources 265

Glossary 267

Index 281

Foreword

As a business owner, you create the future vision for your company, you develop strategies for taking the company there, and then you communicate the actions required for pursuing those strategies. You are the one driving the business to success.

To make this work, you need to understand the unique skills and attributes of your employees and then make sure that you have assigned the right person to the right job to help you achieve your objectives. However, as your business grows, this personal knowledge of your employees becomes harder and harder — at some point, you may not know all of your employees well enough to make the correct judgment calls.

That is where human resources managers come in. They are the bridge between your business strategies and the staff who will execute those strategies. They help you determine your staffing needs, find suitable job candidates, interview them, and then make the right selections. They help draft performance evaluation, compensation and benefits plans, employee motivation schemes and training and career programs to ensure that your employees keep improving their skills and capabilities to match the changes in your business. They protect the employees through discrimination, privacy, and health and safety policies. And when things go wrong, they handle labor relations, discipline procedures, and employee termination. These human resources generalists may seem like miracle workers, but they are the lifeblood of most growing businesses.

But when your business is too small to hire a human resources professional, what then? Most small businesses struggle with human resources issues; some even get in legal trouble for breaking rules they did not even know existed. Workplace law is not a simple subject, and the regulations are changing frequently. It is hard for any business owner to stay on top of it all.

So, what do you do? Do you develop your own human resources skills or hire a human resources manager? The decision comes down to funding and time: Can you afford to pay the salary of a professional human resources manager, and how much time can you afford to waste on resolving human resources issues yourself when you should be focusing on leading your business toward achieving its strategic objective?

If you decide to hire a professional to help, this book tells you how to identify and select an outstanding human resources manager. But hiring one is only the start. Your new manager could just provide the basic human resources services such as employee hiring and management of the compensation system, or the manager could help you direct your employees to fuel growth and profits. You need to decide how to get the most value out of your investment in this professional assistance. *365 Answers About Human Resources for the Small Business Owner* provides you with the help you need to make those decisions: from how to determine whether you need professional managerial help to how to select an outstanding human resources manager and use that individual to help deliver your organizational strategy.

On the other hand, if your business is still in its early stages and you cannot afford to hire professional help, this book provides you with the practical advice you need on many critical topics including finding, interviewing, and hiring employees; compensation, motivation, and performance evaluations; collective bargaining; employee discipline; and much more. Not only do you get practical advice for handling these situations, but you also get an overview of the relevant laws affecting each area so that you can better understand what sets of rules may apply.

Not just another book full of dry rules and statistics, this book is a useful reference guide for experienced business owners and a "crash course" for those who find themselves in a tough situation. Dealing with people is never easy, and it is particularly difficult when the government has crafted so many different laws and regulations restricting how you can manage your staff.

This book helps you navigate the minefield of workplace law and gets you on the course for smooth sailing.

— **Kevin J.J. Aguanno**, *PMP®, MAPM*
Certified Executive Project Manager
Application Innovation Services, IBM Global
Services, IBM Canada Ltd.
IBM Certified Executive Project Manager
IPMA (Level B) Certified Senior Project Manager
IBM Certified Specialist for Rational Unified Process
PMI Certified Project Management Professional

CHAPTER 1

The Role of Human Resource Management

Human resource management is the general term for all of the functions encompassed in the acquisition, retention, development, and administration of a company's employees. This set of functions formerly fell under categories called personnel administration or personnel management. It should, therefore, cover every function in this process, including planning labor needs, job analyses and descriptions, recruitment methods, interviewing and selection, orientation and training, compensation management, records management, performance management, health, safety, morale, fairness issues, and, ultimately, termination, including firing and layoffs as well as retirement.

Why Does a Company Need a Human Resource Department?

Every company must deal with human resource issues. In a small company, the owner probably starts out handling these duties and then may delegate responsibilities to an administrative assistant or someone in the finance department. As a company grows, senior management will realize that many duties require specialized training and background. As more laws are passed that regulate the employment process, it becomes increasingly important for a company to have the expertise to understand and to comply with these laws. An employment-related lawsuit could cost a firm ten times more than a competent human resource manager would. The complexity of employment law and the fallout from not following it properly are often what lead a company to hire a professional to handle the responsibilities of human resource management.

When and how does a company owner or board of directors decide that it is time to establish a human resource department? Usually, this is not a planned decision, but rather a result of normal growth and expansion. A growing business will require additional employees, but it also will require the business head to focus on the core aspects of the business and its growth. When he takes time away from that to advertise, recruit, interview, hire, and train each new employee, his primary duties will suffer. If a small business owner spends entire days interviewing candidates, this is time he is not spending contacting and following up with

customers or clients. If he concentrates on the core aspects
of the business, he will require additional help in the
form of new employees. This Catch-22 is first solved by
hiring someone who can replace the business owner in
performing the hiring function. Many companies, at least
in the beginning, use existing in-house staff. For example,
an administrative assistant places ads and conducts
interviews, and then the payroll clerk handles the
administrative end of the hiring process. This approach
is fraught with potential dangers and will work only as
a stop-gap measure in a growing business. Errors, legal
problems, and continued growth will eventually force
the business owner to hire or to designate an individual
whose sole duty is the human resource function.

The Routine Duties of the Human Resource Department

A company that decides to formalize the human resource
management function by hiring a specialist must consider
applicants with broad ranges of experience in different
areas of the field. Applicants may also have varying
backgrounds, ranging from the former payroll clerk who
worked her way up to department head to the graduate
with a master's degree in labor relations. The level of
knowledge and experience required will depend on the
company's individual needs. Frequently the number of
employees will determine the managerial level of the
HR specialist. A company that employs primarily hourly
blue-collar workers on a factory floor, for instance, will

have different requirements than a medical practice with a staff of professionals. Accurate payroll processing and performance management may be more important in the factory, while compensation and retention management may be more important in the medical office.

The normal duties of the human resource manager, or, as the company grows, the human resource department, covers the full range of employee relations, including some overlap into other departments. To be effective, the HR manager should be a member of the senior management team, participating in the company's overall strategic planning process. This will enable him or her to project staffing needs, design more effective job descriptions, and coordinate training and development programs. He will need to work with other department heads to understand the requirements of each position: with the accountant or controller to develop payroll budgets, with the legal department to ensure compliance, and so on. The position of human resource manager requires a level of responsibility and seniority that will allow him or her to overlay the human resource function onto the entire structure of the organization. Typically, the routine duties performed by the HR manager and the HR department are:

- Planning for labor needs.

- Conducting job analyses and writing job descriptions.

- Recruiting candidates.

- Designing and conducting selection processes.

- Selecting candidates.

- Managing the hiring process (considering job offers, making reference checks).

- Orientation of new employees.

- Developing training programs in conjunction with other departments and then managing these training programs.

- Developing a payroll budget and managing compensation (wages, salaries, and incentives).

- Managing such benefits as health, dental, and life insurance; pension plans; vacation; and sick days.

- Setting performance criteria and conducting appraisals.

- Counseling and disciplining employees, handling labor relations with unions.

- Assuring compliance with relevant tax laws.

- Assuring compliance with relevant employment laws.

- Ensuring the safety of employees.

- Maintaining employee records.

- Terminating employees.

Setting Objectives
for the Human Resource Function

A company that is newly establishing a human resource function should be clear about its needs and requirements. Some companies prefer a strongly centralized approach, in which all HR-related functions are handled only by the HR department. Other businesses prefer line managers to be responsible for interviewing, making the hiring decisions, and training employees, leaving only the administration to the HR department. Making this delineation clear is critical: managers stepping all over one another in interviewing and hiring and the resulting confusion for staff can be disastrous for employee relations. Setting firm objectives for the human resource department can be difficult and, at times, counterproductive, but controls need to be implemented to make this function of the organization as accountable as any other. Does the company want to have limits on how long a position can remain empty? This may mean hiring a less-than-ideal candidate. How closely does the salary budget for a particular department or position have to be followed? Perhaps some "wiggle" room will have to be built into the budget numbers to attract the best candidate. Should quality-control checks be established? These will help ensure, for example, that all necessary forms are completed for each employee, that each employee interview is conducted in the same manner (to avoid inferences of discrimination), and that testing, reference checking, and other pre-employment procedures are done systematically. What kind of error margins can be tolerated? Unlike some line functions objectives, such as product per man-hour, product rejection, and return rate, objectives of the human resource function are difficult to measure. How does an organization say, "Of every 20 employees you hire, we expect 18 of them to be flawless"? Some objectives, however, can be established and measured, and the human resource department will benefit from having a system of measurement. Reduction in turnover rate, increased employee participation in training programs, and a decrease in workers' compensation claims are a few measurements in which accountability on the part of the HR department will increase employee morale and corporate bottom-line profits.

In addition to making and sometimes enforcing personnel policy, the HR department can have a strong role in employee management. The HR manager should make it his or her responsibility to inform employees about policies and changes, and how they affect employees' morale. When an employee feels that his voice is not heard by management, it is the HR department that will hear the complaint and receive the brunt of the blame. Most employee complaints are about pay, benefits, working conditions, and recognition, all responsibilities of the personnel department.

Since the HR department is at the forefront of the hiring process, bringing in top-quality employees should be one of the main goals of that department and of the company. The HR department also frequently has the ear of the general staff. Problems and concerns are usually brought to HR first. A first-rate HR manager will use this information to alert senior management of problems that are simmering, before they become full-blown fires.

Confidentiality must be respected, of course, and the HR manager does not want to assume the role of company spy, but both general staff and management will benefit if the HR department is attuned to falling morale, overworked employees, or complaints about supervisors. The HR department may be responsible for the employee training and development, influencing the future growth of the company. In today's customer-focused environment, well-trained employees can mean the difference between success and failure.

The HR manager and his department should be informed of new developments in personnel management. Technological advances, trends in hiring practices or benefits programs, and changes in salary structures or demographic shifts in the labor pool should all be brought to senior management's attention as part of good corporate governance. Especially in the field of labor law and regulations, any changes should be investigated and acted upon quickly.

The HR department should also stay abreast of such

changes in computer programs as payroll processing, employee management databases, training software, and other programs intended to enhance efficiency and lower costs. The dizzying array of products in this field makes it difficult to judge which are the most valuable, but an HR manager should be familiar with new developments in HR management software to make informed decisions or recommendations to management.

The human resource department can also be instrumental in managing and monitoring quality-control programs in the rest of the organization. Because quality-control programs depend on well-trained, motivated the HR function and quality-control are closely linked. If the HR department makes it a priority both to establish and enforce performance standards and to support those standards with excellent training programs, the quality-control function will be easier to manage. The HR department is responsible for incentive and reward programs and can integrate them into processes, motivating employees to perform better. Frequently, departments are graded on their adherence to quality-control measurements. The HR department can devise incentives for meeting all goals, meeting 95 percent of goals, and so on, effectively spurring the department to better performance that will meet the quality-control goals.

The HR department also can design and develop comprehensive employee involvement programs, a major productivity booster. At the outset, the HR department conducts new employee orientations. This is a perfect time to start new employees on the path of becoming involved. If employees are informed from the beginning that their involvement is valued, and the entire company in cooperation with the HR department follows a policy of inclusion through team building, feedback and assessments, and worker empowerment, then productivity and quality will surge.

Qualities of an Outstanding Human Resource Manager

Choosing the right person for this job not only will be the greatest challenge, but also will result in the greatest value for the company. An efficient, well-run, caring human resource department is the life blood of an organization. Employee morale has a great impact on how successful an organization becomes, and employees who feel valued, respected, and rewarded (not only monetarily) will have good morale. Regrettably, many employees view the HR manager as the evil character Catbert in the Dilbert comic strip, arbitrarily issuing and applying policy and being an obstructionist at every opportunity. The HR department must view the employees as its customers; HR is there to serve the employees, and therefore should be working as a good customer service department would, assisting in any way possible within its scope of responsibility. A good manager will train his or her staff in good customer service, and an HR manager should be no different. Hiring a poor or even incompetent HR manager will result in a broad range of serious problems, including having unqualified employees, high employee turnover, lost time in interviewing, legal issues resulting from discriminatory actions or unsafe conditions, decreased morale and motivation, and poor training. Today's sophisticated and educated workforce requires and expects efficient management of employee rights, benefits, compensation, and career development. In addition, the highly regulated nature of business requires an HR manager who is familiar with local, state, and federal issues that affect personnel management, and who is sensitive to the diverse needs of today's workforce, including flexible schedules, family management issues, and benefits packages.

In theory, skills applicable to the human resource field can be quantified as well as verified. Many colleges and universities today offer programs in human resource management, and there are independent certification programs such as "Professionals in Human Resources" and "Certified Benefits Professional." Education and certification may assure a company that the candidate has the technical skills for the position, but experience in managing the HR function is critical for outstanding performance. How does a company find an outstanding human resource manager? In general, a combination of the educational level and technical skills necessary for the level of the position, combined with a number of years' experience, preferably in the same industry, will yield a competent HR manager. The critical skills for a human resource manager, in addition to HR credentials, are sensitivity and integrity for dealing with difficult and personal issues, and good oral and written communication skills. Some proficiency in mathematics and computers is desirable and can be measured, but how do you gauge sensitivity, integrity, and communications skills in finding the ideal human resource manager? Asking the right questions in the interview process will be a great help in this area. Good interviewing skills will pay off in all hiring decisions, but especially when hiring an HR manager. Keep in mind that an experienced HR manager is also an experienced interviewer and probably knows the answers his interviewer hopes to hear. Nevertheless, it is important to ask the traditional, "Tell me about yourself" question to check for sincerity and to learn his or her philosophy of HR management. Find out if the candidate knows about your company, and, more importantly, if he or she shows a genuine interest in it. Ask about skills and strengths in prior positions and how they can help your company attain its goals. Focus on what the candidate considers his or her most significant career-related achievement.

Another interview foil is to present a negative hypothetical situation for the applicant. The candidate's reaction and proposed solution can frequently give the interviewer insight into the prospect's management style. Did he propose handling the situation in a sensitive manner? Was she all-business in her approach? A final aspect to examine is whether the applicant shows the general management strengths the company is seeking. If the company has decided that the HR manager should be an integral part of the senior management team, he should not be so much of a specialist that he cannot make recommendations and decisions on a company-wide level.

A superior HR manager will make it his business to keep abreast of new trends in the field and to offer new solutions to the company. If a prospective HR manager is a member of relevant professional organizations, seems well-read in his field, and can offer novel solutions to personnel problems the company faces, he will probably be a good choice. Too many people in this field become stagnant and get used to doing things the same old way.

As a company grows, a full-blown HR department may be required, and the duties of each staff person in the HR department will become more specialized. A large company would typically have a vice president of human resources, aided by an administrative assistant, and then a veritable army of specialists including a director of employee health services, a manager of compensation services, a manager of employee relations, a director of benefits services, payroll processing clerks, employee counselors, recruiters and interviewers, job analysts, training specialists, and so on. An outstanding human resource manager, in this case, will also have to be a good department manager, able to train, motivate, and guide his or her own staff.

Ensuring that the Human Resource Function Is Integrated into the Overall Corporate Strategy

The human resource function has undergone tremendous

changes during the past 15 years. One of those changes is the recognition that the HR function has to be an integral part of the overall strategy of the company. The human resource practices and policies of a company directly affect the performance of a company because they directly affect the performance of one of the company's biggest assets: its people. Because of this, the human resource function has assumed more business importance in the modern company. The most senior employee involved with human resources should have the ear of the top echelon of management or even be a direct member of senior management—not in a supporting role, but with input into the financial, operational, and strategic planning of the firm. The HR specialist helps formulate long-term staffing strategies and designs training programs that ensure proper performance of jobs, features necessary to the survival of the firm. This increased role has led to a field of study now known as strategic human resource management, which links human resource management with strategic goals and objectives to improve business performance and develop organization cultures that foster innovation and flexibility" (Truss and Gratton, 1994).

It is not surprising, then, that most progressive companies today actively include the HR role in developing and integrating their overall corporate strategy. In order for this corporate level strategy to filter down to the everyday functioning of the organization, it must be built into the hiring process, the training process, the retention process, the safety process, and many others. For this to happen, the HR manager needs to know not only what the plans of the company are, but also to have an active role in formulating them. For example, if a company is looking at widening its market focus to the immigrant community, the HR department will need to understand recruiting for bilingual staff. As a firm develops or adopts new technologies, the HR manager will need to understand the basics of the technology to attract qualified technicians. If a company has identified that it needs to develop a more diverse workforce, the HR function has to spearhead those efforts. In other words, the HR department has to adapt HR practices to fit the company's larger goals in its corporate strategy. To be able to do this most effectively, human resource management must take a broader view of the business than has been traditional and should be a partner in both formulating and implementing the company's policies.

CHAPTER 2

Developing a Personnel Policy

Why Does a Company Need a Personnel Policy? Should It Be in Writing?

Every company has a personnel policy, whether it is published or not. Once employees are told they must arrive a 9:00 a.m., they have an hour for lunch, they get two weeks of vacation each year, and they can join the company's group health insurance plan, a personnel policy has been established. The decision to develop a written personnel policy usually is inspired by the same factor that prompted the decision to form a human resource department—the growth of the company. At some point, the small business owner realizes he cannot answer all the questions concerning personnel issues that continually arise, so he decides to put as much of it on paper as possible, allowing the employees to answer their own questions. It is considered wise to document any policies that have been followed to avoid problems later. If a policy is not documented, it may be applied differently to different employees, raising questions of discrimination. The company's personnel policy should not be confused with mandatory postings of federal and state laws governing certain employment issues.

With a clearly stated written policy, a company can be consistent in its decisions regarding salaries, schedules, promotions, and discipline. In the absence of a personnel policy, supervisors or managers make their own judgments on these issues, leading to inconsistent and possibly illegal decisions.

Employees tend to believe they are treated fairly when there is an official document stating that each employee will receive the same treatment. If a company has a clearly written policy that both forbids discrimination and harassment and outlines disciplinary procedures up to and including termination for offense, the company will be in a better position to defend itself against charges of discrimination.

There is a wide range of interpretations as to how a company's personnel policy should be written, and there is an almost limitless list of choices on how to define, write, and structure a policy. Often a company's employment policy already exists in some form. A general guideline is that a personnel policy should answer the questions employees routinely ask about their employment and responsibilities. Some companies cover the broad topics, while others have long and complex policies that address every known contingency. Including only as much information as is needed will foster fair and even-handed treatment of employees, making the department manager's jobs easier by answering many of the questions for them.

For the sake of brevity, the policy should not contain information contained in other publications, except perhaps in a general overview. If an "official" procedure is not routinely followed because employees have found it expedient to handle it a different way, the company would be hard-pressed to enforce noncompliance as grounds for termination, but it is important that the policy does not become a straitjacket for the company, allowing no room for discretion or creativity in management's dealings with staff.

Most companies seek a balance between a policy that covers every conceivable contingency and one that is so broad that it offers no guidance. In either case, the policy has to be clear and easy for both employees and supervisors to interpret. The primary purpose of the document is to inform employees what is expected of them and what they can expect in return. It should be an employee-friendly document written in understandable, everyday language, using a positive tone.

Legal and Other Pitfalls
in Developing an Employee Handbook

Employment policies were initially compiled as a means
of keeping employees informed. However, employees
can misconstrue them to be an employment contract
or guarantee of employment, providing the policy
is followed. To avoid this, most companies include a
disclaimer indicating that the handbook or policy is not to
be considered a contract of employment, but is intended
as a guide. Furthermore, it is not a complete description
of the company's policies. Today, both employers and
employees use handbooks and personnel policies as tools
in adversarial relationships. Employers use the policy to
prove that an employee broke a rule he or she should have
known about, and employees try to interpret wording of
the handbook as promises the employer is legally bound
to keep. It is not a contract. A contract is an agreement
by two or more parties *with some value exchanged*, to do
something for the other. If you expect the employee to
abide by these rules, what is the value exchanged for them,
a guarantee of employment? The value exchanged is not
the employee's salary; salary is exchanged for the labor
performed. A company has to be careful in the wording of
the policy to make sure that there are no implied contracts
and that no part of the policy violates law. In a few
cases, certain clauses in employee handbooks have been
construed as a legal contract of a guarantee of employment
to the employee by the employer. Statements regarding
length of service could be implied to mean a contract of
specific length. Also, using the expression "termination for

cause" can create an implied contract. The understanding being that if there is never any "cause," employment is guaranteed. It is always wise to have an attorney review a personnel policy, checking to see that the policy has adequate disclaimers regarding guarantee of employment, that the policy is a source of information only, and that the company reserves the right to make any changes it deems necessary.

A company should consider using a professional service to develop its policy. These services provide a basic policy that can be modified to meet the company's individual needs. A company may also consider purchasing an off-the-shelf personnel policy computer program. Because this type of policy manual has been reviewed by an attorney, the company is assured that it will not be in violation of any employment laws by following it, providing the program meets the approval of state employment laws.

The personnel policy should also allow for changes. A disclaimer to this effect is also necessary, stating that the policy can be changed by the company president or board and that any new version replaces previous versions. For this reason, the personnel policy should not contain information that is subject to frequent change. Once policies have been formalized in writing, there is an obligation to apply the policies consistently.

Any disclaimers contained in the personnel policy should be repeated in a number of places in the handbook. In addition, they should be stated in bold or italic print.

Costly lawsuits and warnings to the contrary, many employers still make implied promises to their employees.

Mistakes to avoid

- **Statements regarding retention.** Such statements as "We want to retain our employees, and if you follow these simple rules…" should be avoided. This employer may have wanted to send a positive, optimistic message about his good intentions regarding employee retention, but he is inadvertently telling his employees that if they follow the rules, they will be retained as employees.

- **Improper language regarding classes of employment.** Do not create a class of employees called "permanent" when you actually mean "full time." The company may view these terms as the same, but a court may rule "permanent" to mean unlimited duration. Do not refer to "probationary" periods as there may be an implication that once the employee has passed "probation," he or she is guaranteed employment.

- **Promises of any sort.** Avoid making any promises of training. If an employee believes that she has not received adequate training (and then is terminated for failure to properly discharge his duties), she or her lawyer can argue that she did not receive the guaranteed training. The same would apply to initial assistance to new employees. Every employer likes to say that the company plans to make new employees welcome and to give assistance in adapting to their new environment, but supervisors frequently fail in this duty when they have their other responsibilities. Statements that imply that new employee assistance *will* be supplied erode the company's position if it has to terminate a new employee. She will say she was unable to do the job because she was not given the assistance promised. Avoid including any promises that the company may not be able to keep, such as annual raises or bonuses.

- **Carefully outline disciplinary procedures.** It may seem like a logical and fair policy to use specific steps in disciplinary procedures leading to termination. However, if you outline in the policy that warnings will be sequential in the form of oral, written, probation, and suspension before termination, you will not be able to fire an employee without following all of the steps. Do not promise a grievance hearing; if the employee does not receive one (perhaps he was dismissed on the spot because of gross misconduct), it can be construed as a breach of contract.

Avoid including any procedures or policies that are difficult or impossible for the company to enforce. And most important avoid using phrases that may be interpreted as discriminatory.

Introduction and Distribution of a Personnel Policy Handbook

A good personnel policy can introduce and support a company's objectives and can give employees and supervisors the guidance they need. It can introduce the company to new employees by stating the company's objectives and by describing how the company sees the employee as part of those objectives. In this way, the policy will be viewed as a tool for everyone involved to achieve the company's goals, rather than as an arbitrary list of rules to be followed. Whether the policy should be issued as an "official" handbook that can be carried around or issued as a more formal document that is kept on file and referred to as needed is a decision for the HR manager. Obviously, a handbook is physically limited in the amount of information it can contain. A company should require that employees return the personnel policy upon termination, a requirement that is more easily met if the policy is kept on the company's premises. Another solution is to post the personnel policy on the company's intranet. In this way, it is fully accessible to all employees and yet stays in the hands of the company. Provisions will need to be made to allow employees who do not routinely work on a computer to access the company's intranet.

It is critical that the personnel policy be introduced and distributed in a fair and consistent manner. If the policy is newly formed, it is advisable to have a company meeting to introduce it to the entire staff. Many companies will have employees sign off that they have received the policy to ensure that each member received a copy and agrees to abide by the policies contained in it. When a policy is questioned, no one wants to hear "nobody told me that." In case of any legal disputes, the employer has proof that the employee received the policy and agreed to abide by it.

When the personnel policy is introduced, explain to the employees that this is not a new set of rules but rather a formalization of the rules they have been successfully following all along. On the other hand, if the company is using the new handbook as an opportunity to introduce new employment policies, it is advisable to have a summary or cover letter informing the employees of changes or additions. When a new employee joins the firm, the introduction, along with a short review of the policy, should be part of the orientation procedure. Note that it is not mandatory to give each employee a copy of the policy. Many companies opt to have the policy explained at orientation and then advise new employees of where it is kept on-site. If an employee loses his copy, he will have to refer to a centrally located one. This eliminates the common problem of employees stating they didn't know the policy because they "lost the handbook." The company should explain that the employees are required to familiarize themselves with the policy and to seek clarification, if needed.

The personnel policy will include, at a minimum, the following topics:

- ·A welcoming statement by the owner, CEO, or

board of directors.

- A statement of the company's objectives, philosophy, or mission statement.

- Attendance policy and hours of work.

- How official information will be communicated to employees.

- A code of ethics.

- Confidentiality policy.

- Personal conduct, including use of alcohol or drugs, abusive behavior, and smoking areas.

- Dress codes.

- Information on how employees are paid (time clock or sign-in sheet).

- Definitions of classes of employment (exempt, non-exempt) .

- Overtime policy.

- Equal Opportunity statement.

- Policy regarding use of company time for personal affairs.

- Resignations, including necessary notice.

- Sexual harassment policy.

- Any necessary requirements regarding drug and alcohol testing, and physicals.

- How personnel records will be maintained and who can access them.

- Security and safety policies and procedures.

- Benefits and, if applicable, eligibility periods.

- Policy regarding time off, leaves, and holidays.

- Policy on performance appraisals.

- Problem resolution and discipline policy.

- Termination procedures.

Personnel policies should be reviewed periodically. An annual review is preferable, but any major changes in the corporate or legal environment may necessitate an earlier review. All changes should be communicated to the employees in the form of a supplement in such a way as to ensure that the newly changed policy has been received, is understood, and will be adhered to, just as the original policy was.

The most important aspect of a personnel policy is that all of the concerned parties understand and follow the policies contained in it. The policy should be introduced at a staff person's orientation, reiterated by supervisors who have a thorough knowledge of it, and applied as consistently as possible. Nevertheless, many employees consider that much reading a bore, never even looking at the policy until a situation arises for which they need information. A company that is truly interested in increasing awareness and understanding of its personnel policy should make a concerted effort to bring that message to the employees. Some companies allow new employees to offer a review or critique of a feature of the policy at orientation; some companies offer role-playing scenarios in which a situation was introduced and the newly oriented employee had to find the solution or answer in the employee policy handbook. Whatever methods are used, the company should underline its commitment to making sure all employees understand the policy.

While a company's policy is usually written by top management, the board of directors, or a bank of lawyers, it is the department heads and supervisors who are burdened with the responsibility of implementing and enforcing it. Once senior management is prepared to support the policies, it is vital that middle managers, the ones who have to deal with it every day, understand the policies, support them, and are properly trained in interpreting and implementing them. It is they who plan the work and vacation schedules, approve days off, enforce lateness and absence policies, do the appraisals and make recommendations for raises, and, eventually, take the flak when an employee is unhappy with any of these.

One way to support department heads and supervisors is by creating a training program in the implementation of personnel policies. When a policy is written for the first time, in addition to "selling" it to staff by holding a company-wide introduction meeting, a company should have the HR department run separate training sessions for frontline supervisors to teach them how to interpret the policies and the best ways to apply them. A great deal of psychology is involved in applying rules, and a supervisor who has the attitude of "that's the way we have to do it because that's what the book says" will not reap the same benefit from the personnel policy as one who has been trained to explain the rationale of a given policy and the reason it has to be applied in a particular situation. Each time the policy is amended, new training should be given again, to general staff for basic explanations as well as to supervisors for in-depth training in interpretation and application. Supervisors who become "experts" on the personnel policy by studying it in this focused way will be able to answer questions and solve problems on their own. This training has manifold benefits: it will stimulate creativity in problem-solving abilities on the part of the managers, it will reduce the burden of the HR department since fewer problems will be referred to them, and supervisors will grow adept at solving small personnel problems before they become big ones.

A personnel policy that is well-written and sensibly applied will become one of the company's most valuable management tools.

COMPANY: New Horizons Community Credit Union

Linda Konstan, Vice President of Human Resources

Our company currently has 65 employees. We have a full employee handbook and other policies with which each employee must comply. If any of our employees has a problem, he or she can go to anyone, including our CEO, who is available to anyone at anytime.

All employees are informed of our policy regarding Internet and phone use, and we provide one week of training on procedural topics and compliance. We run very lean, so it's up to the employee to show initiative to be trained to advance.

We perform criminal, DMV, employment background, and bondability checks on all candidates. In addition, we may perform a credit check depending on the job.

Our official company communication method is usually in meetings or by e-mail, depending on the scope of the topic. We have an open-door policy. Managers hold meetings. The vice presidents walk around, so our employees get to know them and vice-versa. Human resources is also out there all the time.

Linda Konstan, Vice President of Human Resources
New Horizons Community Credit Union
99 South Broadway • Denver, CO 80209
303-744-3535 • www.newhorizonsccu.org

CHAPTER 3

Job Descriptions— Know What You Need Before Your Interview

Staff Planning

Employment planning is one of the most important parts of a company's strategy. Any expansions the company intends to make, any new markets it expects to enter, and any new facilities it aims to build or acquire will require a plan as to how to staff the positions to meet these new goals. Many variables will enter into the strategy. Personnel needs are usually determined by forecasting the revenues that the new venture will raise. This, in turn, will determine the size of the staff required to generate this volume of revenue. Then the skill requirements of the staff must be determined. A major new project will require both line staff and additional administrative staff, or at least additional hours by the existing administrative staff. A company will analyze whether it wants to hire from within or recruit from outside of the company. If staff are moved within the company, they must be retrained for new duties, whereas outside recruiting would stipulate that candidates must have the necessary skills for the position. In a large company, staff for the new project can probably be culled from an existing database of all employees with relevant skills and backgrounds. In a smaller environment, department heads and supervisors know the skills of their workers and should be relied on for their input. The analysis will focus on the size of the pool of available in-house candidates versus the general labor pool. In a tight labor market in which the availability of highly skilled workers is limited, it may be wiser to moved skilled staff internally, providing additional training. If the skills required for the new positions are abundant in the labor market, the company has an opportunity to fill the new positions with trained staff.

Another reason for staff planning is to determine whether increased business has created the need for additional staff and whether the staffing need is temporary because of some short-term market forces or if it is a trend that will continue. For short-term needs, having employees fill the void by working overtime or by using staff from other departments may be the best staffing plan. Another option is to hire temporary staff. Workload analysis studies can be used to determine staffing needs. These studies determine how long it takes to do the necessary task multiplied by how many times that task has to be done with the current production volume. As long as volumes are not temporary, this analysis will determine additional or reduced staffing needs.

A staff analysis will further assist a company by determining the duties required for the company to function and by then projecting how many staff and what kind of staff will be required to perform those duties. It will also help in defining which characteristics a company may look for in each position. An analysis such as this would typically entail examining all of the work activities the company requires to produce its products or services, the human behaviors necessary to complete these activities (selling, typing, making phone calls, operating a conveyor belt), the tools and equipment the company needs to supply to its staff, the standards that have to be met for the company to function, and the required skills that have to be incorporated into all of these activities and factors.

Having clearly defined job descriptions will prove invaluable. In all of the above cases, the HR manager must know what is required of the person filling the position. If staff are transferred internally, the requirements of the new jobs may be compared with existing job descriptions. The HR manager can then arrange for the training necessary to fill any gaps. If you recruit from outside, the parameters for the job can be set for the recruiters and interviewers to use. If a company is expanding, it is especially critical to develop job descriptions for the new positions that are developed. Taking on new staff without a clear idea of what each new staff member is hired to do is bound to lead to failure and frustration for both the company and the new employee.

Organizational Chart

It is important to know where the positions that need to be filled fit within the company's organizational hierarchy. Certain positions may require technical expertise alone, but many technical positions — for example a senior engineer — may have staff report to him or her, requiring additional experience or training in supervisory skills.

The organizational chart shows how work and responsibilities are divided and how each staff member in a company relates to the others. Staff may have direct reporting relationships with one another, or they may work with one another laterally, as peers in different departments whose duties overlap or are integrated. Even small companies can benefit from having organizational charts. Starting at the top, the chart should outline who reports directly to the president, who reports to each of his subordinates, managers, or department heads, and finally to the staff who report to these middle-level employees. An organizational chart will help a new employee see how each position in the firm relates to the others as well as where he or she fits.

Developing the Job Description

Many of the hiring mistakes companies make are the result of not having a clearly defined description of what the company really wants the new applicant to do. A well-written job description should assure that all parties involved, including the head of the company, the applicant, and the supervisors, understand what the position entails and share the same expectations. A job description will not only inform an employee about the company's expectations of him or her, but it also will help managers to supervise and appraise performance and determine compensation categories. As the basis for the hiring decision, the job description should be discussed with all candidates. A precise job description will assist interviewers by keeping them focused on the duties of the job and skills required. Job descriptions will continue to be valuable in appraising performance and further developing staff, but the description's utmost purpose is as the key building block of the hiring process, securing the right candidate in the right job. In addition to assisting in recruitment and selection, the job description will help guide the company's management in determining proper compensation and in developing training programs to meet the standards set in the job description.

Obtaining the information for developing a job description is called job analysis. Large companies may have industrial engineers or human resource analysts do this, but smaller companies will rely on middle and upper management to determine what will be included in the job description. The primary questions management should ask when developing job descriptions are: Who should write them? What is the source of the information? How will the information be used? Determining how the information will be used will answer the other two questions. If a company wants to use the information for planning staff growth to meet corporate growth, line managers must supply the information regarding new products, services, and markets. If the descriptions will be used to formulate a training and development program to meet new challenges or improve functions, the training and human resource departments will provide most of the input. If job descriptions are being written for the first time for existing jobs, the best sources are the employees doing the jobs. This can be as simple as asking the people who perform the job to walk through the steps they take to get the job done. During such an interview, the person responsible for writing the job description asks a series of questions that would build to a total understanding of the job under analysis. These questions would include what kinds of education, training, or experience are necessary for the job; to whom they report; who reports to them; what kind of equipment and skills are necessary for the job; what standards are used to make sure the job is done properly; and what other duties they may have outside of the core job.

A job description for a new position will be best written by the department head for that position. If the new position is similar to existing jobs, the job analysis as described above should produce the details needed. Frequently, a new job develops as a support or assistant position to an existing one, and the core of the new job will have responsibilities similar to the existing one. In this case, the supervisor or the person for whom the assistant is designated would be the one to provide input for the job analysis. His or her perspective of the position and how it would help in his or her own job should be the basis of the new job description. A workload analysis can determine which new duties have been created that produce the need for the new job, or which duties need to be shifted, easing the burden on the original job-holder.

The Basics of a Job Description

The job description should include:

- **The job title**. The level of seniority of the position will frequently determine the title of the position. In addition, because so many jobs today involve multiple duties, it is more difficult to put a label on a particular job. In the past, a secretary took dictation and typed letters. Thanks to new technology and management styles, the secretarial position has evolved into that of an administrative assistant who handles a great many more duties than just sending out letters. The title of the position should reflect as many of these duties as possible, without becoming an unwieldy label.

- **The person or persons to whom the position reports.** If there are multiple reporting duties, each should be clearly defined, so supervisors do not each expect exclusive claim to the staff person. The person or persons who report to this position should also be made clear. In addition, any individuals outside the company that the person may be required to work with should be identified.

- **The responsibilities of the job.** Every aspect of the job cannot be covered, but its essential responsibilities and duties should be delineated. The descriptions should not be too general, however. For instance, if you simply state that the position requires computer literacy, when you really want someone to be able to work with spreadsheets or do desktop publishing, then you will not have listed the skills required. If the position requires covering other positions during certain peak seasons or during vacations, this should be part of the job description. The EEOC (Equal Employment Opportunity Commission) lists a number of factors that should be considered in determining which responsibilities are essential: amount of time spent in the function, how often the function is performed, what happens if this responsibility is not performed, and what previous employees in this job did. These factors should be included to determine the priorities of the job as well. The description should not be merely a list of responsibilities; rather, it should also reflect which duties are of primary importance and which are secondary.

- **Required skills and education.** Included are special training, certification, or licensing, as well as such specialized skills as computer entry, mathematical ability, and the ability to speak a second language. Skills that are difficult to quantify — good communication, attention to detail, the ability to work under deadlines — also should be included in the job description. In some civil service or union jobs, the specifications are strictly spelled out, and deviating from those specifications could have legal ramifications. Be sure that the requirements are truly required.

A company may prefer to have a Certified Public Accountant (CPA) as its chief accountant, but for a private firm, that is not mandatory. An auditing firm, however, can only use CPAs to conduct an audit, so this certification is a requirement for them. A college degree in a particular position may be desirable, but vast experience in the field may be more valuable. Many firms address this issue by requiring a mix, so that numbers of years on the job will substitute for a degree. Demanding a rigid mix of education and experience will narrow the field of qualified candidates. A job specification that allows for some flexibility and growth will probably serve the company better in the long term. Be careful of requirements that may be construed as discriminatory. Make sure it is a bona fide requirement of the job, able to be proved or demonstrated that it is required. For instance, a job that demands heavy lifting must be described only as "ability to lift over 60 pounds."

- **Required experience.** Not only should the length of previous experience be specified, but also the type of experience. Determine whether it is important that the experience is in a particular industry, or if experience in a related field is acceptable. For example, a clinic may want a nurse with public health experience, but a hospital may simply want five years' experience working as a registered nurse in any setting.

- **Working conditions.** The applicant has the right to know that he or she may be working in a high-pressure, noisy, or dangerous environment. If the position requires any physical labor or physical skills, then that should be outlined in the job description.

- **Performance expectations.** When such clear-cut criteria as "accurate posting of daily A/R and A/P entries," or "accurate data entry of approximately 5,000 files per day" can be applied to a position, use these descriptions. Goals should be clearly stated, and expected results or main objectives should be delineated. However, in many administrative or professional positions, these criteria are difficult to define and quantify. Nevertheless, a job description should include the company's expectations for the position so that substandard performance can be addressed and so that the employee can monitor his or her performance.

- **Salary level or grade, if applicable.** Many companies use pay grades or pay ranges to address the issue of fairness in compensation. Under such a system, the organization groups jobs of similar levels of authority, responsibility, and skills into pay categories.

A job description should be as realistic as possible. It is unfair to build a "dream job" of all the things you would like to see done in that position. The job description should focus on the position as it should be, not reflect what is done by the current employee. People subtly and gradually change jobs to suit their personalities, and a position can evolve completely from its original intent. In some cases, this may mean that the jobholder assumes more responsibilities, and in others, the jobholder shifts some responsibilities to other employees. Of course, jobs change as a company changes, and job descriptions should be reviewed and updated whenever jobs are eliminated, jobs are combined, or a department expands. Otherwise, the description should be reviewed and updated annually. An advantage of writing and systematically analyzing job descriptions is discovering what is not getting done. These unassigned duties are usually noticed only when something falls apart.

To be a truly helpful tool, a job description must be a living document that is referred to routinely for clarification of duties and annually for performance appraisals. It is also instrumental in assisting in the interview process when a position needs to be filled, in expansion plans to understand current duties, and in downsizing scenarios to see which positions may be combined.

CHAPTER 4

The Recruiting Process

Where to Find Staff

O nce a company has a clear idea about its organizational structure and has developed job descriptions to indicate who does what within the company, it is time to start filling those positions. This is job recruitment. The range of recruiting methods is as wide as a company owner's or human resource manager's imagination. A small shop may use the old-fashioned method of putting a "HELP WANTED" sign in the window, a technique that still works well in the retail field. A large organization will probably have to resort to a nationwide or global search for candidates, especially for the top or highly specialized positions in the company.

Today, the most prevalent ways in which companies seek

new employees include:

- Current employees

- Word-of-mouth or employee referrals

- Business contacts

- Help-wanted ads

- Employment agencies

- Executive recruiters

- Internet searches

- Job fairs

- College placement or counselor services

- State job services

- Temporary agencies

Current Employees

Promoting from within is usually viewed as a positive method of filling open positions. It is good for employee morale because it sends a message to the employees that they have opportunities for advancement. It is also a good motivator, encouraging an employee seeking a promotion to pursue additional duties and training. Of course, promoting from within will leave another position open, so it does not save any time, energy, or money for the company. Nevertheless, the benefits outweigh these factors. With internal transfers and promotions, a company is usually assured that it will have a candidate who is not only already trained in the basic tenets of the organization but also has the experience of working within the company mission and philosophy. The employee's work record, both his strengths and his weaknesses are known, and he is likely already committed to the organization.

The most important item to address is that *everyone* in the organization is notified about the open position. Just as with outside advertising, however, a company can stipulate a required level of seniority, training, experience, and education to narrow the field, but the process itself should be as transparent as possible to avoid accusations of secretive, behind-closed-doors operating techniques. Companies frequently post job openings on the company bulletin boards, send out flyers, or post an e-mail message to all employees. Posting an e-mail, however, may exclude employees who do not work on computers, so e-mail communication should be reinforced by a flyer or a poster. It is a mistake to assume that applications can only come from similar departments. Someone in the accounting department, for example, may have a position in sales as a long-term career goal. If such a candidate lacks the required background for such a change, then it is the opportune time for the company to foster morale and motivation by setting the employee on a career-development plan in sales.

The company should have an established procedure for internal applications. Often the employee may have to apply through his or her supervisor, or the supervisor may be asked to recommend his or her employee for the position. These situations can result in problems if there is an adversarial or jealous relationship between the employee and the supervisor. It may even happen that the supervisor values or relies to such a degree on this employee that he or she will sabotage the employee's efforts. Ideally, employees apply directly to the HR department. Many companies maintain databases that list the information from employees' résumés concerning their skills, training, and experience when they join the firm, updating it as new training is completed. If an employee is taking employer-sponsored trainings and courses, these should automatically be updated in the database. It is up to the employee to supply information and proof if he or she receives any outside training and courses. When a position becomes available, the HR department can review the database to find potential internal candidates. This is often viewed as one of the most equitable methods of handling internal applications. Alternatively, the company may request the employee to supply a résumé. The interviewer would use it as a guide in the candidate's interview. Internal transfers or promotions should avoid the appearance of having been staged. It is demoralizing if the company goes through a charade of opening the position to all employees when it already knows who is going to fill the position.

There are some disadvantages to hiring from within.

The employees may not have the right talent for the new position; employees may assume everyone in the company will eventually move up, regardless of talent or effort; and employees who applied and did not get the job may become bitter and disgruntled. If an internal candidate was qualified but not chosen, it is important to offer guidance to improve their chances in the future. Whenever an employee is rejected for an internal transfer or promotion, someone in the organization should take the time to explain, in detail, the reasons he or she was turned down and to offer ideas for career development to ready him or her for future opportunities.

Finally, it may not be in the best interests of the company to rely solely on in-house talent. If all managers come from the same managerial culture, new ideas, new visions, and new types of leadership may be overlooked.

Word-of-Mouth or Employee Referrals

Frequently, especially in a small organization, the owners or managers will post or otherwise broadcast an opening. This may be as simple as, "We need a new manager; does anyone know of someone who may be interested?" Among larger companies, there is often a formal employee referral program (ERP). An employee referral program rewards and recognizes current employees who refer new hires to the company. It is less expensive and usually more reliable than employment agencies and advertising. As a rule, the employee who recommends a friend or relative has a vested interest in seeing the referral do well. ERPs also boost morale by giving employees a sense of empowerment in an area usually reserved for management.

In addition, the referred candidate typically will have a positive image of the company from the person who referred him. When using referral exclusively, watch for charges of discrimination, particularly if all your employees are male and white, and are recommending only their male, white friends and relatives.

Some firms fear that employee referral will lead to nepotism and favoritism. Employees' reporting to close relatives may result in animosity among other employees. The practice of allowing powerful or senior employees to fill positions with relatives, while qualified in-house candidates are ignored, leads to bitterness, not to mention charges of discrimination. Nonetheless, practice has shown that employee referrals are one of the most reliable sources of recruiting new employees.

If a company wants to set up a formal employee referral program, there are some guidelines to follow. Many times such a program will be a simple cash-reward program, but some guarantees should be built into the process to ensure that the program does not create a revolving door, bringing short-lived employees into the company and cash to the referrer. Before such a program is initiated, it should be well planned to avoid this kind of problem. First, the firm must stipulate that the new employee will remain in the position for a certain length of time before the referral reward is payable. Next, determine what rewards the company will offer. Cash is an easy option, but some companies choose to offer trips, extra vacation days, or even restaurant or store gift certificates. The reward program will be less costly than using employment services and advertising.

Good communication and follow-up are essential in a good employee referral program. If the program is not widely known, the number of referrals will be limited and, more critically, the uninformed segment of the employee base will feel marginalized. Establish a formal procedure whereby the announcement of job openings, incentives for referring, and the rewards for success are clear and are communicated to everyone. The guidelines for the programs should be publicized each time a position is opened. Some companies even go so far as to train their employees in the program and encourage them to be effective recruiters for the company in their personal lives. Keep the referring employees informed as to the status of the procedure and let them know their participation is appreciated. Successful referrers should be informed immediately and the awards distributed as soon as possible. Make this procedure as visible as possible to encourage future participation in the program. Some companies choose to limit the employee referral program to positions that are difficult to fill.

It is imperative that the management team is on board with the strategy of employee referrals. Usually the cost benefit of such a program is an encouraging factor. Managers who are concerned they will end up with employees who are unqualified must be assured that applicants introduced to the firm through the employee referral program will receive no preferential treatment over other candidates.

Business Contacts

Businesspeople in similar fields can be an excellent source of referrals for job candidates. If they are also in the interviewing process, they are turning down qualified candidates once they have made their own selection. They may have filled a similar position recently and could forward the additional applicants. They may be able to refer perfectly qualified applicants to you. Companies that may be laying off employees are also a good source of potential applicants. Normally, layoffs are based on seniority, so the company may be forced to let go of qualified employees. Customers, vendors, and professional contacts provide a network that is an effective way to attract applicants. Managers and supervisors should be encouraged to network in the same way. They are constantly talking to and meeting with businesspeople who are good sources of referrals for job applicants.

Help-Wanted Advertising

By far the most well known, and until the advent of the Internet, the most common recruitment tool was help-wanted advertisements. Almost all of the different media can be used. Typically, the local newspaper is the recruitment tool of choice for lower-level positions, including blue-collar, clerical, or service personnel that would be filled by local talent. This tool works fine in fields in which the position has few requirements. Sometimes this type of ad works too well and a company may be deluged with responses, especially in fields that are overpopulated or in an area with high unemployment. Screening applicants for eventual interviews is a time-consuming task. Management positions, especially those requiring financial expertise, more likely would be advertised in a business newspaper such as *The Wall Street Journal*. Positions in specialized fields or that require specialized skills would be more suitably represented by ads in industry journals. Law, nursing, and engineering are among the fields that have professional journals that frequently contain employment advertisements. These journals, however, are usually only published monthly, so the recruitment process is somewhat slower.

An imaginative approach to advertising open positions will probably yield better results. In many instances, entry-level positions can be filled by high school or college students, and advertising in a school publication will attract those candidates. Frequently, a part-time position may be filled by an older, retired candidate. Companies can advertise for older workers in senior-center bulletins or in newsletters for retirement communities.

Newspapers and journals are not the only kinds of media that can be used to advertise open positions. Consider advertising on local radio or television stations to reach a wide audience. Also consider placing an ad in a section of the newspaper other than the classifieds. For instance, a clothing manufacturer might consider advertising in the fashion or style section, while a sports equipment store might place an ad in the sports section to attract the most interested candidates.

What is the best way to develop an advertising campaign to recruit new employees? Keep the goal in mind; writing an ad that would compete for a Pulitzer Prize is less important than writing an ad that will attract responses from the right kind of candidates. A well-written ad should be able to eliminate candidates that do not have the proper qualifications for the position advertised. Filtering the applicants at this level will save the HR staff untold hours in reading résumés or applications. It is better to receive responses from a handful of truly qualified candidates than to sift through hundreds of résumés from people who do not fit the position.

Composing the ad should be fairly easy using a well developed job description. Newspaper and journal advertising is fairly expensive, however, so it is important to be as concise as possible. The main items in the ad should be the job title, general information about duties, required qualifications, something about the company, and, of course, response information. It may be important to describe the inherent nature of the job: fast-paced, a lot of outside contact, working independently, or, conversely, the ability to follow strict guidelines. Be careful in the job title and description of duties; it is important neither to exaggerate nor understate. The ad should convey a sense of enthusiasm about the job, present the job accurately, and attract attention. Ads with borders or backgrounds stand out more than others. It is advisable to place the ad in the weekend edition of the paper; that is traditionally when job seekers check the classifieds. Consider pacing the review and interview processes by running the ad, skipping a week, catching up with the résumés received, and then advertising again. The responses received may offer insight into how to improve wording in the ad. It is possible to combine ads for two positions to save money, but they should not be completely disparate. For instance, the ad for the controller should not be included in the same ad as for the mail clerk.

Be clear about the response technique preferred and tailor it to the type of position. Consider accepting résumés for technical or more senior positions by e-mail. Reply to all respondents, even if they are not considered for an interview. An alternative is a "blind ad," in which the company is not revealed, and newspapers supply a box number for responses. Requesting faxes can sometimes serve the same purpose, but Internet search features allow people to search based on telephone or fax numbers. Finally, carefully proof the ad before it is sent for publication. A misplaced digit on a fax or phone number will send hundreds of résumés to an unknowing individual.

Employment Agencies

To avoid the hassles and potential legal complications of directly advertising open positions, many companies will choose the more expensive route of using an employment agency. Employment agencies usually charge one percent of annual salary, with caps for higher salaries and with guarantees for length of time in the position. If the new hire is not working out at the three- or six-month mark, depending on what was negotiated, the fee is refunded.

When considering using an employment agency, look at the available budget versus the time available to devote to filling a position. Writing ads, placing them, screening applicants, and conducting interviews are time consuming, and that is why so many companies choose to work with employment agencies. Although these agencies may be expensive, a cost analysis of time spent by staff involved in recruiting may prove worth it. Unless a company has an HR department with trained professionals, the staff to whom the job falls may not be up to the task. As a result, the company may hire the wrong person for the job. Frequently, an employment agency is a final resort after a company has tried unsuccessfully to fill the position itself. If an agency is used, it will pre-screen the candidates based on the requirements. Then the HR manager sees only the most qualified.

Employment agencies have more experience and better expertise in writing and placing ads that will attract the right candidates. Frequently, an employment agency will specialize in one or two fields, medical or clerical for instance, and will be able to offer the top-level candidates from their roster of applicants. In addition, an employment agency will keep information private. After working with an agency once or twice, it will be more attuned to the company's needs, perhaps offering further assistance. An employment agency also can contact currently employed individuals who would not normally be in the pool of applicants.

An employment agency is not infallible. It has to make assumptions about the company that only the staff may know. It has a vested interest in filling the opening as quickly as possible to reap its fee. Know the agency; someone should take the time to sit down with the recruiter who will be responsible for the account and acquaint him or her with the company and its needs. Make sure the company's recruitment needs are clear. In addition, make certain the fee schedule and any guarantees are agreeable. If the agency is sending candidates that are unacceptable, restate the company's needs and requirements.

Executive Recruiters

Also known as "headhunters" or "search firms," executive recruiters work exclusively with high-level executives, including CEOs and CFOs. They usually work on retainer and are paid for the search even it is unsuccessful. Usually, candidates for these high-level positions are not actively seeking employment, and the executive recruiter has the contacts and expertise to approach this kind of target. Executive recruiters also may specialize in the financial field or in the technical field, further intensifying their range of contact and expertise. Although executive recruiters are expensive, it is assumed that only the top executive or a board member will be involved in the search for a senior executive, and it is difficult to put a price tag on their time.

As with employment agencies, the more the executive recruiter knows and understands the firm, the more successful the search will be. The recruiter should deal with the top staff in the company. The executive recruiter works for the company who retained him, not for the applicant. He will usually contact a small, select group of potential candidates to determine their interest. The identity of the company is not usually revealed until some formal discussions have taken place and an interest shown on both sides. Because the position to be filled is high level, the recruiter should be an individual who can be trusted with sensitive information about the firm's plans, growth prospects, and anticipated changes. Especially if the company is publicly traded, this information can be volatile and should be handled with the utmost confidentiality. The senior members of management or board members should make the decision as to which executive recruiter to hire. In addition, they should interview other clients to make sure the recruiter is able to do a thorough search and handle both the potential candidates and the company properly.

Internet Searches

Almost everything can be done on the World Wide Web today, so it is no surprise that many firms now recruit on the Internet. More than 10,000 Internet sites are available where jobs can be posted. Like most sites on the Internet, they make money through advertising. These sites post millions of jobs worldwide and may not target the desired geographical location. To use the Internet to post jobs, have a plan in place before the need arises to fill a position. Surf the various sites to see which ones suit the company's corporate personality. These sites have a section for companies listed and a section for job seekers; look over the job seekers to be sure the candidates are those the company would want to attract in the desired geographic area. Not surprisingly, computer-related and technology jobs are predominant on the Internet. One of the downsides cited regarding Internet posting is the flood of responses a company may receive. Be diligent in designing an Internet ad to make sure the respondents are viable candidates.

A company wishing to advertise on the Internet might consider having its own Web site; applicants who surf the Internet in their job search will also want to look at the company's Web site. Openings within the company may be posted as a link on the Web site. Candidates may learn about an opening from another source and then decide to research the company offering the position.

In general, online job postings offer a tremendous value for the investment. Compared to other methods, they are relatively inexpensive, give the employer access to a huge field of candidates, and offer quick turnaround in terms of seeking and obtaining good candidates.

Job Fairs

Job fairs are usually sponsored by professional associations or community organizations. The sponsoring organization handles all of the details such as renting the site and advertising the event. Often, employers do not have to pay to attend because the goals of the organization are job growth in the industry or community. On the opposite end of the spectrum are job fairs that are expensive and have the feel of a convention or trade fair. These are usually aimed at technical applicants. Some companies also choose to run ads announcing that they will be at the job fair and that they are "looking to fill the following positions." Job fairs are an effective recruiting event to bring job seekers to employers in great numbers. Many times they are industry-specific, especially when run by a professional association, but they also bring candidates with diverse backgrounds. As in any job posting, be clear when articulating hiring needs. Establish a system of accepting résumés for positions not currently open so that they are available to consider for future openings.

Just as print ads should attract candidates and project the correct corporate image, job fair booths should project that same image. Recruiters should look professional and act friendly and welcoming. Display and informational material should be neat and well organized. Make sure recruiters have been trained in interviewing techniques, avoiding any improper questions. Consider having senior staff visit for an hour or two on a rotating basis to represent the company and lend an air of authority to the event. Pre-screening can be done on the spot if recruiters are well versed in the job requirements of the available positions. Keep paperwork at a minimum, but be sure to collect contact information so that the candidates you are interested in can be reached readily.

Most companies that participate in job fairs are pleased with their success and may take part in more than one a year.

School Placement Services

Especially for large companies, sending representatives to college campuses to recruit seniors has become a time-honored tradition that is an important source of management and technical candidates. However, for the benefits derived, it is expensive and time consuming, involving travel, individual interviewing, and excellent coordination skills. Corporate representatives must be properly trained to handle the interviewing and follow-up. The HR manager or another senior officer should introduce himself or herself to the staff in the college placement office. Once they know the company and its needs, they will be better prepared to refer appropriate candidates. If there is a job opening, alert a college guidance counselor about the need. The counselor may be able to suggest a candidate even before the typical "college interview rounds" in the early spring, providing a head start on the other companies using colleges as a recruitment source.

In interviewing college students, be prepared for a non-corporate culture. First of all, good college students have just come from being trained to challenge ideas and formulate their own. They may question your company's policy on the environment or on social issues. Also be aware of the needs they expect to meet in a career. Typically, they may be a little starry-eyed about how they view their future. Be prepared to present the job offers realistically without bursting their bubbles.

Offering internships to college students before graduation has proved to be a successful technique of recruiting. A company will be able to train an intern in both job skills and corporate culture, learning the intern's strengths, work ethic, and business personality. Many successful businesspeople started out at as interns. Work-study programs serve the same end and give the student valuable experience while supplying the company with relatively low-cost labor.

State Job Services

Every state has a job service under the auspices of the U.S. Employment Service. These were formed during the Great Depression in the 1930s. Today, even during times of high employment, these agencies seek to place the unemployed in appropriate jobs. Their services are usually best suited for recruiting lower-level or blue-collar employees. They offer a large databank of possible applicants and usually will test applicants in the skills or aptitudes they claim to have. There is no fee for their services; they are funded by tax dollars. The disadvantage most employers see with state job services is that they usually represent the most difficult-to-place candidates, including the chronically unemployed. These state agencies, in collaboration with the U.S. Department of Labor, run an online résumé service called America's Job Bank. An employer can either search the job bank for appropriate candidates or submit a job order with the bank, which the agency will try to match.

State services are also an excellent source of personnel who are difficult to place because of a handicap, although they are excellent workers. Financial incentives are frequently available to employers who hire people with disabilities. These agencies will train the candidates in job skills to help them cope in a typical business environment. State offices for the aging also offer recruitment services for elderly workers who are either not emotionally or financially ready to stop working.

Temporary Agencies

As a stop-gap measure, companies are usually successful in using temporary employees to fill an open position. This solution gives the employer time to conduct a thorough search for the position, while assuring that the job will continue to be done. Most temp agencies are able to offer a wide range of highly skilled staff with the necessary training and abilities to handle the job. In the past, these kinds of positions were limited to clerical or administrative assignments, but today they range from highly technical to blue-collar jobs. Employees are specifically tested, so the company using the service can count on the temp stepping right into the job, with perhaps a little training in the company's specific methods. Frequently the company is so satisfied with the temporary personnel that he is hired as a permanent employee. If this is a possibility, it should be made clear to all concerned. Some temps do not want a permanent position either because they enjoy the freedom of taking time off periodically or because they enjoy the challenge of different jobs.

Temporary employment may seem expensive to an employer, but many times when the costs of all of the benefits of a permanent employee are added to his or her salary (taxes, health insurance, vacation days, retirement benefits, and so on) the additional cost is minimal. Additionally, though it is not common knowledge, the competition among temp agencies makes it imperative that fees are negotiable.

Testing

The main purpose of employee testing is to keep the
hiring process as objective as possible. There is a wide
range of tests and types of tests from short quizzes that
are supposed to detect candidates' honesty to complex
tests to confirm proficiency in certain skills. Tests
can be conducted in-house, but there are also testing
organizations that perform this service.

The main types of tests are intelligence, aptitude,
performance, and personality. Aptitude tests or basic
skills tests are designed to test the applicant's ability
in a certain area, usually technical in nature. Typing,
computer, and mechanical tests are examples of aptitude
tests. Performance tests are more specific in that they
test the applicant on the particular performance required
in the position. A translator may be asked to translate
a passage or an advertising executive might be asked
to write some advertising copy. It is difficult to test for
general managerial skills, however. Personality tests are
used to gauge whether or not the applicant has the right
qualities for the job at hand. Their true value as a hiring
tool is controversial, however, and they should only be
interpreted by professionals in that field. Whatever test or
combination of tests is used, the company administering
the tests should be extremely careful to give the same
test under the same conditions to all applicants. Doing
otherwise may be construed as discriminatory. The EEOC
and the Department of Labor have issued guidelines for

the use of tests as a selection measure:

- The ability being tested must be relevant to the performance of the job.

- Tests should be validated to ensure fairness.

- Scoring must be fairly and consistently applied.

- Tests must not create a barrier to the disabled.

A large company may have the staff and expertise to analyze a job, design or choose the appropriate tests for it, and then administer and validate it fairly. Many smaller companies do not have this kind of ability and need to be careful in the use of screening by testing.

Selecting for Interviews

Usually the first screen for selecting candidates for the interview process is a review of résumés or applications. This review should be done by the head of the department filling the position and someone in the HR department. Each should study the job description and compare the requirements in terms of education, experience, and skills to the applicants' résumés. The department head should know what kind of background and skills are needed in the position, and the HR representative should be able to give further insight into acceptable salary ranges and benefits to be offered. To save time on the part of interviewers, the first screening may take place by phone.

If you have a list of requirements that are not necessarily covered in a résumé or application, a phone screening will narrow the list of candidates. Remember that many applicants will be currently employed, so the phone interviews may have to be conducted outside of business hours. This is also the time to let the candidates know they will be contacted only if they are scheduled for an interview to save countless hours of staff time devoted to answering questions about the status of the position. This is also the time and place to address the salary requirements. Some companies request or even require applicants to include their salary requirements with their applications. If this is not done, the applicant can be asked his or her salary range during the phone interview. An applicant who is way out of range should be screened out at this point.

Applicants who are not being considered for the position should be sent a polite note thanking them for their interest.

Once the résumés or applications are reviewed, a file or database should be set up for the "short list" or finalists. Depending on the number of applicants remaining, the company may want to add an additional screening step or start to schedule interviews.

COMPANY: Auxiliary Services Corporation

Michelle K. Brackin, Human Resources Manager

We employ 175 full- and part-time employees. We also employ 200 college students who work ten hours per week during the academic year. In addition to a written personnel policy and written job descriptions for each employee position, we have an organization chart in the employee handbook. We also review the chart with new employees at an orientation session held each semester.

To recruit candidates, we use newspaper ads for nonskilled, entry-level positions, while we use the Internet for professional positions. We are a small organization with limited advancement; however, we do encourage and give some preference for internal candidates.

To determine whom we will interview from the résumé pool, we review the applicants' education and experience to make sure they meet the minimum requirements. We then review for the type of experience needed in our industry or for the education and the skills needed for the position.

The supervising manager conducts the interviews for non-skilled entry-level positions. For professional positions, the interview is conducted by a committee of managers, and, in some cases, an invited union representative.

We really want to get to know the candidates during the interview process, so we ask several questions to gauge their personality, including: Tell us about a time you had to deal with a difficult
customer or co-worker? Tell us about a time when you had to
make an ethical decision, where doing the right thing would have a
political price? Tell us why you left each of your previous employers.

In addition to the interview, we contact previous employers and
co-workers listed as references. We check Department of Motor
Vehicle Records for drivers. We also use a Reliability Indicator
Questionnaire, and we require copies of college transcripts for all
positions requiring a degree.

> *Michelle K. Brackin, Human Resources Manager*
> *Auxiliary Services Corporation*
> *Neubig Hall SUNY Cortland • Cortland, NY 13045*
> *Brackinm@cortland.edu • Ascweb.cortland.edu*
> *Phone: 607-753-2431*

CHAPTER 5

Interviewing Candidates

The employment interview is one of the chief screening tools companies use in selecting personnel. The job of interviewing is an art and a science, and it is difficult to do well. Yet, in most companies, almost anyone in the company can be and has been given the duty of interviewing candidates.

Who Should Conduct Job Interviews?

Most managers who are responsible for conducting job interviews have never been trained to do it properly. Even in the cases of those who are trained, conducting interviews is a duty that is not routine unless the company has high employee turnover. Nevertheless, it is necessary to include employees who are not professional interviewers in the process if they will be affected by the decision. A company must identify all of the people who need to be part of the hiring decision, but that does not mean that they should be involved in interviewing. It is important to get different perspectives on an applicant, but having too many individuals (in the case of panel interviews, for example) directly involved in the interview itself can be daunting to the applicant and can bog down the hiring process. You may use one-on-one, sequential interviewing, but an effective and time-saving technique is to use two interviewers.

If a company has an HR department, someone in the department should be the lead interviewer, assisted by the manager or a supervisor for the department with the position to be filled. This dual involvement will help the interview be more balanced, and it also gives each interviewer breathing room and time to make notes. These notes can be compared afterward to create a more objective viewpoint of the candidates. Some HR departments have hiring managers who are competently trained in interviewing. Most of the time, the human resource personnel handle interviews in addition to their normal duties. However, there are many sources and guidelines for explaining proper interviewing techniques, and a competent HR manager will make sure he or she has studied many of them.

Any company that decides to use some of the more aggressive interviewing techniques, such as situational interviews (the candidate has to role-play handling a problem or crisis), behavioral interviews (the candidate has to supply situations where he or she handled problems in the past), and stress interviews (the applicant is treated rudely to judge his or her reaction "under fire") should be careful to use well-trained, professional interviewers. (These aggressive interviewing techniques are discussed at length in *Human Resource Management*, 9th Edition, by Gary Dessler, Prentiss Hall.) A company should avoid using the most loquacious individuals in the company to handle the interview. The idea is to find out about the candidate, not about the interviewer. Having the interview conducted by two people, one of them from human resources, should alleviate this problem, since the HR interviewer should be able to re-establish the direction of the interview.

Training the Interviewers

Because of the many sensitive issues involved in interviewing, it is imperative that any staff who will conduct interviews be well-trained, enabling them to determine a candidate's suitability for a job in the shortest time.

Everyone who will conduct interviews on behalf of a company must know which questions should not be asked. Interviewers may not ask questions directly regarding a candidate's age, marital status, nationality, race, religion, health, or sexuality. In addition, interviewers must avoid asking questions that may be *construed* as discriminatory. These would include:

- **Questions that might give an idea of the applicant's age.** An interviewer may be seen as fishing for the information if he or she asks when a candidate graduated from high school.

- **Questions that pertain to an applicant's nationality**, such as "That's an unusual name, where does it come from?"

- **Questions about whether an applicant rents or owns his or her home.**

- **Questions about organizations.** Membership may indicate religion or nationality.

- **Questions about health**, aside from, "How are you today?" This category includes the question, "When is your baby due?" (even if the candidate is obviously pregnant).

- **Questions about other languages spoken**, unless they are a bona fide requirement of the job.

Many companies have found it easier and safer to develop an applicant interview form for the interviewer to complete. Such a form can help to keep an interviewer on track, and it assists in making sure all important and relevant information is gleaned from the interview. It even helps the company to adhere to anti-discrimination laws by making sure the interview technique is consistently applied. Even with a standardized form, however, the interviewer must be trained both to move the interview along at a measured pace and to read the subtle clues conveyed in an employment interview. A good interview form will contain standard questions about prior experience, examples of work done, and accomplishments achieved, but it also will leave room for interpretive questions that will allow the interviewer to have some real insight into the candidate.

Controlling the Interview

If one looks at a typical interview, it is easy to see why it is not the favorite duty of most managers. It is often as uncomfortable for interviewers as it is for candidates. It is important for an interviewer to maintain control at all times. Often, especially in fields where aggressiveness is an asset, as in sales, for instance, the interviewer may face a candidate who tries to direct the conversation to achieve his or her own ends. Too many interviewers, because of their discomfort with the process, tend to discuss pleasant topics instead of dealing with the facts at hand. In order to maintain control, interviewers are wise to take a few steps in advance to assure a smooth interview:

- **Be prepared.** Know the requirements for the position and read the applicant's résumé beforehand. Have an extensive knowledge of the company's corporate philosophy, personnel policies, and the general organization.

- **Make sure the interview will not be interrupted.** Close the door and have calls held or redirected.

- **Make the applicant comfortable** and start with small talk. Introduce yourself! It's surprising how many interviewers leave out this important step. Make sure the applicant knows that you will be taking notes.

- **Use an interview questionnaire** to see how the applicant's background relates to it. If your company does not employ one, design one to use. Know the job description and ask relevant questions about the job.

- **Schedule enough time** to allow the applicant to complete any application or paperwork required as well as any tests the company administers.

- For most employment interviews, **allow about an hour** and divide the interview questionnaire by increments of time so that you can remain on schedule. You may want to put your watch on the desk to keep an eye on the time without having to crane to look at a clock or constantly check your wristwatch. Allow a few minutes for candidate questions. Review and explain how any follow-up will be handled through additional interviews or testing. Inform the candidate that a decision will be made shortly.

- **Know the objectives of the interview.** Yes, it is important to know as much about the applicant as possible, but only as it relates to the position. Consistently remind yourself of the attributes and talents you require from the applicant. Assess maturity, integrity, and honesty as well as performance in past positions. In addition, present the company in the best possible light to a good candidate.

- **Pay close attention to what the candidate says**, but don't allow the applicant to do all the talking.

- **End the interview on a positive, polite note**, thanking him for his time. Stand and lead the applicant to the door, so that it is clear the interview is over.

- **Allow time to review your notes** and to make comments before preparing for the next interview.

If you recognize that an applicant is not a good candidate, it is wisest to inform him or her right away. Cite whatever has disqualified the candidate, saying, for instance, "I'm sorry, this position requires extensive experience in designing and working with Excel spreadsheets."

Ask the Right Questions

Most interviewers know what kind of information they want to obtain, but do they know the right questions to elicit that information? There is no formula or list of the right questions, and most managers have to develop their own based on the position. An HR manager may develop a company-wide interview questionnaire. In either event, the right questions have to be determined. Questions that can be answered yes or no should be avoided; the object is to get an in-depth look at the candidate.

If you have carefully read the application or résumé, do not waste time asking questions about the applicant's history. Here is a sampling of questions that may be used to gather the most relevant information from an interview:

- What do you know about our company? What makes you want to work here?

- Why are you considering a job change?

- What do you feel are your strongest and weakest points? (Ask for elaboration and examples.)

- Which of your skills and strengths would be of the most value to our company? (Focus on relevant skills. Discuss computer software used, projects managed, how a budget was developed.)

- Are you a team player? (Ask the applicant for examples.)

- Describe how you manage multiple tasks and deadlines.

- Tell me a little about what you do in your current position.

- What factors have most contributed to your career success?

- How do you manage conflict? (Ask for examples.)

- Have you been involved in the expansion of a business? If yes, what was your involvement?

- How do you deal with difficult people to whom you have to report?

- How do you deal with difficult people who report to you?

- Here is a hypothetical situation that can occur in this position; how would you handle it?

- What do you consider the most important contribution you have made during your career?

- Where do you see yourself in three, five, ten years?

"Tell me about yourself" is one of the most familiar interview questions, so many candidates will have a pat answer, making the question of little value in obtaining deeper insight into the candidate's abilities.

If the candidate is less than forthcoming in his answers, do not assume he is withholding information. He may not think on his feet quickly (and if that is important, this is the time to find out). He may be shy about past achievements. Wait a moment or two for answers. Most people cannot tolerate silence for too long and will respond. Obviously, not all of the questions will be asked in every interview. Some questions will lead to information that cancels the need for a different question. In addition, some responses will take longer, necessitating the need to eliminate some questions. As long as both the same list of questions is used as a guideline and no discriminatory questions are asked, there should be no problem about unfair treatment. The most important factor in avoiding discrimination suits is consistency in the application of policies, including interview policies.

The Hidden Interview

Often an interviewer's intuition will indicate that a certain candidate is the right one for the job. Reading the résumé and application, asking the right questions (and getting the right answers) will lead to that feeling, but the interview should confirm that the candidate has the qualities listed on his résumé. Is he enthusiastic, does his intelligence level meet that of the position, and does he seem competent? Does he seem to enjoy talking with people, if it is a people-oriented position; conversely, does he seem the type to enjoy working alone doing research or lab work if that is what the position requires? If you have thoroughly acquainted yourself with the job, you should be able to gauge the suitable personality for it.

Be aware of some of the traps of the hidden interview, however. Make sure it is the applicant and not an idealized version of the applicant that is appealing. Beware, for example, of the so-called halo effect. Many times, some aspect of the candidate will so impress the interviewer that it colors all of the other aspects of the interview. This may be his appearance, a degree from an impressive business school, or membership in an organization the interviewer admires. Another trap to avoid is hiring a candidate simply because he or she thinks along the same lines. It's human nature to admire people who are like us, and many candidates are good at "reading" interviewers and giving them the answers that they expect or want to hear. Also avoid being immediately impressed, or unimpressed, by a candidate's initial presentation. First impressions are lasting, yes, but an interviewer must realize that the core of a candidate's qualifications must be examined.

Interview Notes

If a company has developed an interview form with suggested questions and procedures, it usually will have included a section for notes and impressions. While the information is fresh, the interviewer should take the time either to complete this section or to write out his notes in some other format. A grading scale may be used so that each candidate can be compared to the others, or the interviewer may just mark his notes with his impressions. This is one reason that interviews should be paced properly; an interviewer should take the time as soon as is practical after the interview to review his notes, add his impressions to them, and file them for later review. After all interviews have been completed, these notes will form the basis for the short list of candidates for the position.

First, personal characteristics should be noted. Most of the time, the interviewer will not be able to discreetly make notes regarding this subject, so it should be done immediately after the interview. Comment on appearance (neat, professional); poise (calm, nervous); manner of speech (articulate, clear, organized); interpersonal skills (friendly, eye contact); and cooperativeness (followed questioning, was not aggressive). Do not use disparaging expressions as memory aids. Remarks along the lines of "fat one in green dress" serve no purpose in judging the qualifications of the candidate for the job. If a candidate's appearance is clean and neat, remark only on that, not on any physical attributes. Of course, if the candidate is not clean and neat, that should be noted as well. It is expected that a candidate will put her best foot forward for an interview, so if she arrives at the interview disheveled, it does not bode well for future conduct.

Reread your notes after the interview and make further clarifications if necessary. Consider using a scale or a grade here to make the comparison with other candidates easier. Your notes should be attached to the résumé and application of each candidate for later review. Each reviewer's notes should be identified and filed. The two interviewers may compare notes and winnow the list down further based on their combined opinions. When interviews are complete, a meeting with the people who will make the final decision should be scheduled, allowing the interviewers to present the best candidates and the reasons for their opinions.

A great resource for interviewing tips and possible questions is 501+ Great Interview Questions for Employees and the Best Answers for Prospective Employees, available from Atlantic Publishing, www.atlantic-pub.com; Item # 501-02; 1-800-814-1132.

COMPANY: New Horizons Community Credit Union

Linda Konstan, Vice President of Human Resources

We have job descriptions written for each position in the company that we review with employees at performance appraisal time. We conduct most of our recruiting through Monster.com and local associations. We determine whom we will interview based on the applicants' qualifications. In some cases, we use assessment testing and behavioral interview questions.

Generally, the hiring manager conducts interviews, although sometimes a team of managers interviews. Three important questions we ask all candidates are: Tell me about a situation you wish you had handled differently based on the outcome. In what way(s) do you express your personality in the workplace? What was the most challenging situation you've faced in your career?

Linda Konstan, Vice President of Human Resources
New Horizons Community Credit Union
99 South Broadway • Denver, CO 80209
303-744-3535 • www.newhorizonsccu.org

CHAPTER 6

The Hiring Process

Hiring the best employees is one of the most important aspects of a successful business. The right people must be doing the right job, or the business simply will never be entirely successful. By following the steps in Chapters 3, 4, and 5, an HR manager will have determined the organization's staffing needs; determined how to attract the most viable candidates to meet those needs; and finally, determined, via the interview process, the candidates who will be offered positions.

Today's complex legal, financial, and training requirements make it imperative to hire the right people. You will lose an inordinate amount of the company's time, money, and effort if the wrong person is recruited, hired, and trained for a job. In addition, a bad hiring decision may cost customers, damage equipment, or create additional work for other employees. Finally, a bad hiring decision will cost in termination fees, including unemployment, mountains of paperwork, and possible wrongful dismissal suits.

Keep in mind that the entire world of hiring has changed radically over the past few decades. In the past, if someone didn't work out in a position, you could either find something else for him to do or get rid of him. Today's sophisticated technical requirements mean it is difficult to move people from one position to another (although, cross-training, especially in small companies, has many advantages, particularly in periods of high production). In addition, letting someone go today requires more than a handshake and "Sorry it didn't work out." Regardless of how short a time a person was with a company, there will be paperwork requirements to be met.

Making the Decision

Most businesspeople pride themselves on their ability to make decisions. Deciding on the right product or service and choosing the right target market are the core of starting most businesses. Businesspeople make thousands of decisions on a weekly and even daily basis regarding production schedules, shipping methods, décor and furniture, salaries, employee training, and so on. Most believe they are perfectly competent to make the hiring decisions for their company. The problem is that most people will rely on their own decision-making skills. Although their "gut feeling" for products, customer needs, corporate image, and the rest may always be on target, in the legally sensitive area of hiring personnel, relying on intuition may not be in the company's best interest. Granted, there is always a "corporate personality" that will work best in your firm, whether he or she is down-to-earth, a traditionalist, or an innovator who shoots from the hip. However, when the definition of the ideal employee is too narrow, it eliminates qualified people and may be inadvertently discriminatory.

A better solution is to approach the hiring process in a systematic manner. Make sure potential candidates meet the criteria set for the position, and then gather as much information as possible on each candidate through interviewing, testing, and personal observation. Make an inventory of each candidate's abilities, strengths, weaknesses, and personality traits. This will help in maintaining an objective view of each candidate and avoid the dangerous trap of letting personal biases make decisions. Many companies have done analyses of their "star" employees in the hopes that they can identify those elusive characteristics that separate the good from the great. Then they can replicate the formula in their hiring practices. How well this system will work is unknown, but the hope is that applying consistent logic in deciding who are the best candidates will yield the best possible results in hiring decisions.

What are the tools one can use in establishing this logic?

The first and most important one is to find out what was done right when hiring certain employees. First examine what kinds of personalities have worked best in the past. Many people will make the assumption that a top salesperson will be a good talker, a real raconteur, to keep his or her customers happy. Reality might have shown, however, that those salespeople who were good listeners and sympathetic to customer needs may have generated the most sales. A medical office may be under the delusion that they have to have a sensitive "people person" at the front desk, whereas the fireball who schedules appointments effectively, keeps paperwork moving, and handles the billing efficiently may be the one who keeps the patients happy. Relying on stereotypes to fill positions may be self-defeating. Find out what really works, not merely what is expected to work in terms of the type of person you need in a position. If you have done this kind of research, you can try to duplicate your top staff when choosing new staff.

With this in mind, decide what characteristics to look for in the interview. A candidate's résumé may have outlined his education, experience, and skills, but it is in the face-to-face meeting that much is learned. Excellent interview notes, with a mind toward the position being filled, will help you to stick to the objective, systematic approach you want to follow. The first impression the candidate makes should not be the deciding factor; rather the determinant should be how well the candidate's personality matches the job's ideal personality. Develop a blueprint for the ideal candidate delineating the most desirable education, experience, skills, personality traits, and characteristics. With this blueprint in hand, you should be able to compare each of the blueprint ideals to the qualities each candidate possesses. Clearly this is the most democratic way of choosing and, if you have defined the job's requirements properly, the most successful.

The second tool a company can use to choose the right candidate is testing. In some fields this is still considered a controversial screening option, but it is one way to be certain a candidate has the requisite skills. Test results are quantifiable and leave subjective judgment out of the equation. These tests measure such things as mechanical ability or clerical skills; in other words, how well the applicants can do the job. In certain areas, this is a reliable tool: a financial analyst should be able to demonstrate certain skills in spreadsheets; an administrative assistant should be able to type a letter in a word processing program and use a scheduling database; and accounting or bookkeeping skills can be demonstrated by making some mock entries. There are also positions in which the ability to lift or carry a certain amount of weight may be integral to the performance of the job. All of these types of tests are considered basic skills tests.

Another type of test that has been developed is the "soft skills" test. For example, a potential customer service representative may be given a test that determines a general attitude toward helping people, and another test may help determine if a candidate is detail-oriented. There are also psychological tests that are intended to identify certain personalities. These tests range from a simple inventory of questions to sophisticated tools that may be administered by a psychologist. These tests are intended to discover personality traits that would identify a person as a potentially good or poor employee. It is difficult for a lay person to use these types of tests properly because they require a great deal of insight into psychological profiles and interpretation.

These tests may be created in-house, or they may be purchased, designed by a testing company and then administered by the hiring company. Thousands of these tests are available today. If a published test is used, however, the company should make sure to purchase legitimate tests, preferably approved by the American Psychological Association. A company may also choose to send candidates to a testing organization off-site.

One of the most important considerations in administering tests is that they are relevant to the job. A second consideration is that they are administered uniformly; in other words, be sure that all of the conditions under which the test is taken are exactly the same for all candidates.

For any of these tests to be truly useful, they need to be marked and validated to avoid discrimination. The EEOC has issued guidelines for the use of tests:

- The activity tested must be related to the performance of the job.

- Employers are encouraged (though not required) to

validate results. This means that the test has been proven to be free from cultural, racial, and sexual bias.

- The scoring system must be clear to the candidate and applied uniformly.

- Either using a purchased test administered uniformly or using an outside testing organization should ensure that the guidelines of the EEOC are met.

Other tests that are used with less frequency (and regarded by many with some skepticism) are handwriting analyses, which are based on the premise that relevant personality traits are reflected in a person's handwriting; integrity (honesty) tests; and lie-detection tests. The use of lie-detector tests is restricted. An employer cannot require that anyone take them and may not terminate an employee for refusing to take one.

Checking References

A careful review of all of these tools — the application or résumé, the interview, and any tests you have decided to use — can lead to an intelligent choice among the candidates. Yet, a prudent company will conduct a number of pre-employment checks on its short list of candidates. It is simply more practical and economical to limit reference checking to the most viable candidates. The reference checks typically done include:

- Professional or prior employment reference check

- Credit check

- Criminal check

- Verification of driving record

- Verification of educational credentials

- Verification of licensing credentials

Professional or Prior Employment Reference Check

One of the first things to be aware of concerning employment reference checking is that, in today's litigious employment environment, many former employers are reluctant to give a negative reference for an applicant for fear of a lawsuit. Many companies today simply give neutral references, supplying only the title or duties of the position(s) held and the length of employment. To circumvent this problem, consider asking for a reference from the employee's supervisor or co-worker, rather than from the personnel department. This may not be possible since many companies have policies that require employees to refer all reference requests to the HR department. There have been some efforts to indemnify former employers from retaliation in the case of a negative reference, especially since there have been some cases where a "negligent reference" has led to the employment of a dangerous or unstable individual. It is a difficult situation. An employer has an obligation to other employees and to his or her customers to be diligent in checking the references of potential staff, but on the other hand, former employers are concerned about defamation of character lawsuits.

In the case of neutral references, at the very least you know whether the candidate held a position related to the one offered, and perhaps you can assume that if the candidate was with the company a substantial length of time that he or she was a reasonably good employee. This is far from foolproof, however, since many companies are loathe to let people go and will hold onto a poorly performing employee well beyond a reasonable length of time. If you are persistent, you may get some questions answered, such as whether the employee had a good attendance record or whether the employee performed to the standards of the company. A simple question to ask, one that only requires a yes or no answer is, "Would you hire this employee again?" An interesting gambit recommended by Richard Fein in *101 Hiring Mistakes Employers Make* is to use the information that the candidate has given to elicit information. For example, comment on how successful the candidate was in improving company sales figures. A former supervisor will likely be compelled to set the record straight.

Another way to obtain information about an employee is to use your own network of contacts. In specialized industries as well as in upper management, everyone seems to know everyone else, or at least know of them. Asking business contacts, customers, or members of the local chamber of commerce or professional association may provide some objective information on the candidate.

Credit Checks

Checking on a potential applicant's credit history will be considered necessary only if the employee will have some kind of fiduciary responsibilities. If an employee with be handling cash, payroll, and accounts payable or receivable, as well as performing controller or accounting functions, an employer has legitimate reasons for obtaining credit checks. Some truck driving positions, notably beer and liquor delivery, may also warrant credit checks, since the driver has access to large quantities of expensive goods.

Criminal Checks

Criminal record checks also can be done on potential employees. These checks are warranted for positions in which funds are handled as well as for positions that require the employee to have unsupervised contact with customers or property, including security guards, apartment supervisors, and others who may have access to homes. Making a hiring decision based on someone's criminal record when no security issue is involved may be considered discriminatory.

Verification of Driving Records

If driving a company vehicle is one of the responsibilities of a position, a check should be done on the applicant's driving record. Most insurance companies will provide an "abstract" of the record. As a matter of fact, many insurance providers require that each of a company's drivers be approved as a condition of the company's insurance policy.

Verification of Educational Credentials

This is one of the most essential and basic of reference checks for potential candidates. The position offered may only require a high school diploma or equivalent, but to ensure consistency, the company should check that each applicant for a position has the educational requirement demanded.

Verification of Licensing Credentials

Many positions require a license to practice in that field. Hospitals or medical centers hiring registered nurses or licensed practical nurses, home care organizations hiring certified home health aides, and public accounting firms hiring certified public accountants are a few examples. Each candidate for such a position should be able to exhibit a copy of his or her license to the employer. The employer will be required by its own credentialing organization to prove that each of these employees has the proper license.

Now that you have this information about a candidate, what do you do with it? If you find that an applicant has completely falsified an important aspect of his background, inform him that this is the reason the position is not offered to him. What if he "overstated" his responsibilities or production in a former position? If you simply view it as the way the candidate was selling himself, you may not have much of a problem with it, as long as his core skills for the position are adequate. If, however, you are uncomfortable that a candidate could have given such an exaggerated version of himself, you may not want to continue with the hiring procedure.

If it is too burdensome to do any or all of these types of reference checks, there are many companies that specialize in this field. They may do only one or two of the checks, or they may be able to run all of the reference checks you need.

It is important that the candidates know that their references will be checked. The simplest way to do this is to include a signoff for it in the application. In many cases, this will discourage unqualified candidates from pursuing the position offered. In such cases as credit and school records, or if you use an outside firm to perform these services for you, the candidate must give his or her written permission to request records. Make sure that candidates realize that performing reference checks is not an offer of employment.

Making the Offer

Once the hiring decision has been made, the job offer is

the final step in bringing the new employee on board. Typically, the salary range will be discussed at some point during the interview process so that both the candidate and the employer have a good idea of salary before the offer is actually made by letter or a phone call. Even when the offer is made by phone, it is advisable to confirm it in writing. It is recommended that the offer is made formally, so there is no room for misunderstanding. Make the offer as quickly as possible after the decision has been made; an exceptional candidate has a lot of options open to him or her and may be considering more than one offer. The person making the offer on behalf of the company should have a thorough understanding of all levels of compensation, including the base pay and bonus or incentive programs as well as benefits provided. The person representing the company also must know what kind of salary discussions took place at the interview. Any additional details, positive or negative, should be included in the offer. Such perks as use of company cars or a sign-on bonus are mentioned, as are such expectations as reporting to headquarters once a week. Give the candidate a firm deadline for replying to the offer and be clear about any contingencies the offer may have, such as drug or alcohol testing (see Chapter 15). The easiest and simplest way to do this is to send the offer in writing and enclose a second copy for the candidate to sign and return.

How aggressively should you pursue a candidate who seems a bit reluctant to accept the offer? This depends entirely on the job market and the exceptional qualities of the candidate. If the position is difficult to fill because of a scarcity of candidates with the qualifications for it, a company may sweeten the offer to qualified candidates through an increased offer or a sign-on bonus. This kind of situation may arise when there is a shortage of graduates in a certain discipline. This has recently been happening in the nursing profession. If there are no other qualified candidates, an HR manager will probably need to be more aggressive in the offer. If, however, other closely or equally qualified candidates are available, the decision will be easier. Another case in which the job offer becomes a highly charged issue is when the candidate is a "star" in his or her industry. Top salespeople are frequently wooed by many companies once they have decided to switch jobs, and a bidding war can ensue. The same is true of certain types of programmers in the computer industry.

Lastly, do not forget about those applicants who were not chosen. Those who were eliminated in the beginning of the process when you were reviewing résumés, for example, should be sent a form letter advising them that "their qualifications do not match your needs at this time," or something to that effect. If you used a blind ad, you will only have to respond to those individuals whom you contacted and interviewed. Avoid outright rejection of candidates; things may change. Send a letter of rejection as soon as you have eliminated a candidate; it is not polite not to keep a candidate dangling, and you or your staff will waste a lot of time taking calls from interested candidates whom you have no intention of considering.

A wise HR manager will hold onto old applications and

résumés and even create a database with them. Be sure to purge the database periodically because the information will become outdated. Applicants who have been short-listed for a position may be sent a different letter, giving a little more detail about the fact that although their qualifications were good, someone with qualifications more closely suited to the position was chosen. Do not discourage this group of candidates, in case something goes wrong in the reference process, or in case something else happens after the chosen candidate has been hired. Consider waiting to send rejection letters until the reference process has been completed on your successful applicant, but do not delay too long. It is frustrating for a candidate not to know where he or she stands.

Mike Smith, SPHR
www.mikesmith-hr.com

Human resources and the hiring manager interview candidates. In some cases, however, a number of managers or professional staff in the hiring group conducts the interviews. Among the many questions we ask, three are the most important: What was your greatest accomplishment? What was it that you added to it specifically? How did you learn how to do it?

A vendor checks previous employers, education, certifications, and driver's license, if the job requires driving. We offer employees 100 percent tuition reimbursement in addition to a 403(b) and a company-funded retirement plan.

New employees at all levels can participate in many training courses and an on-site mini-MBA program. When new jobs open, we post the positions internally.

To keep employees up to date with company news, we use intranet news, "broadcast" voice mails, a newsletter, and quarterly all-staff meetings where the president gives a status report on our company. Additionally, we solicit employee feedback by conducting an annual employee survey.

> *Mike Smith, SPHR*
> *Six Sigma Certified Black Belt*
> *www.mikesmith-hr.com*

CHAPTER 7

Orientation, Training, and Career Development

The most successful new hires are those who are made to feel as though they are a part of the company before they actually start working. Once the job offer has been accepted, someone at the company should get in touch with the new employee before her start date. More than one person may be in contact with her, which is even better. Someone in the benefits department may send out enrollment paperwork and then call to see if there are any questions. The department supervisor or assigned mentor may send an orientation schedule with a note saying that he or she is looking forward to meeting the new hire. The president of the company may send a packet with a welcome letter, corporate information brochure, and annual report. If, as is often the case due to reference checks and required notifications to former employers, it will be a few weeks before the candidate starts, sending these correspondences out on a staggered schedule will keep the new employee informed, making this transition process smoother. The continued role of orientation should be clearly delegated to someone in the company.

A supervisor, mentor, or member of the HR staff should be assigned to the new employee to guide her through what can become the maze of a new company. The supervisor or mentor may consider calling the candidate a day or two before she starts to let her know where she should park, whom she should ask for at the front desk, and to brief her on the dress code. Various staff may have parts of the orientation of a new employee assigned them, but the overall coordination of this effort should lie with one responsible person. If the mentor or other responsible person uses an orientation checklist, he or she can check back with the new employee from time to time confirming he is on track with her orientation. A good idea would be to review and update this checklist so that any interim changes in procedures are reflected.

Picture a new employee who is welcomed at the front door by her supervisor or mentor, led to a desk that already has her name plate on it and her telephone and computer set up with her name and temporary passwords. She then has an appointment with the HR department for benefits orientation and with a member of the security staff for a badge, photo, key code, and emergency-evacuation orientation. Contrast that with the employee who waits in the reception area for a half hour until someone is found to bring him to his desk, then sits at his desk until his supervisor comes out of a meeting and tries to show him what he is supposed to do in the middle of a constant stream of phone interruptions, while an administrative assistant runs around to find him a pencil and pad for his desk. Which employee is impressed with her new company? Which employee is more likely to give his best effort back to that company in reflection of the efforts made for him? All too often companies put a great deal of effort into recruiting and hiring good candidates, only to leave them "hanging out to dry" on their first day at work.

A comprehensive and well-designed orientation program sends a positive message to employees that the company is willing to invest its time in them. It also gives the organization the opportunity to explain goals, mission statements, and corporate philosophy to new employees.

Benefits Enrollment

Most of the time, the benefits that a company offers will be discussed, at least in a general way, at the interview. For most people, it is critical to know whether their health insurance coverage has a waiting period of one month, or if they will have to continue paying COBRA for a three-month waiting period. Provisions for retirement, stock options, or 401(k) plans may become the deciding factor in whether or not a job is accepted. In cases where the job market is tight, qualified candidates may be shopping around for jobs based not only on salary, but also on the overall package of benefits offered. It is important, therefore, that interviewers are aware of any tiers of benefits that are offered, waiting periods, choices between benefits, and so on. For instance, it can be disastrous for a new employee to find out he is not eligible for the dental plan for a few months when he or she has a child who needs to have orthodontic work done right away. If this is the case, you may have to deal with a disgruntled employee who has already lost some confidence in the organization.

A corollary to being clear with the employee regarding benefits during the interview process is being diligent with the employee regarding benefits during the enrollment process. A member of the HR team who is thoroughly familiar with the forms should be responsible for assisting new employees in completing them. The forms should be checked thoroughly for accuracy before they are processed so that no benefits will be affected adversely. Any HR department with the attitude that it is the new employee's responsibility to make sure all of his or her benefit paperwork is completed sends a clear message that it is an uncaring, corporation that the employee has joined.

It is important that a significant block of time be allotted to benefits enrollment during an employee's orientation. Many companies offer so-called "cafeteria" plans that allow the employee to choose from various options available. He may waive a health insurance plan if his spouse has ample coverage, choosing a medical reimbursement plan instead. Perhaps he is offered a 401(k) matching-contribution plan with different matching levels from which to choose, and he needs to know the tax implications attributable to each level. To anyone but a benefits expert, these choices can be confusing and overwhelming.

Usually, at the same time as the benefits enrollment, a staff member of the HR or payroll department will set up the new employee on the payroll system. Close coordination between HR and payroll is critical, since the human resource department will be obtaining such information necessary for payroll as marital status; exemptions for withholding and W-2 purposes; payroll deductions for health, dental, life, or other insurance; and employee match deductions for savings and 401(k) plans.

Dress, Conduct, Confidentiality

Companies are still entitled to require a certain level of dress decorum if they choose. Many companies today opt for casual attire in the workplace, but casual attire may be allowed only in the back office, where employees do not meet customers, but not allowed for the receptionist or salespeople. Some companies have opted for "casual Fridays," and some may allow casual dress for most days except for those when meetings with corporate staff are scheduled. If a company does choose a casual dress policy, it is important that the elements of it are clearly spelled out. Typically, most casual dress policies will disallow jeans, sweat pants and tops, jogging suits, slippers or sandals, shorts, and midriff or halter-type tops. Sometimes, even when a casual dress policy has been adopted, exceptions may be made for working in certain areas. Sandals or open-toed shoes may be allowed in summer, but not for employees who work in the stock room, for example.

Employers do have to be careful about exhibiting discrimination in dress codes, however. For the most part, requirements that employees dress conservatively are not considered in violation of Title VII of EEOC rules, as long as they are applied consistently. However, requiring women to wear white blouses and dark skirts, for instance, while only requiring men to dress conservatively, would be considered a violation. Similarly, a business that requires women to dress in a provocative uniform while not requiring the same of men may be charged with discrimination.

Most issues of employee conduct are questions of common sense and good manners, but a company may be compelled to spell out limitations on certain behaviors. Cursing or telling off-color jokes in the workplace is covered under sexual harassment regulations, but loud or abusive behavior that does not cross those lines may also be discouraged officially. The recent preponderance of "constructive dismissal" or "hostile work environment" lawsuits are forcing companies to look at how employees treat one another. Companies may also have conduct rules that apply to public image issues, including the way phones should be answered or if correspondence needs to be reviewed before mailing.

A company may have a policy regarding confidentiality concerning customers or clients or proprietary information owned by the company. Confidentiality agreements are frequently required if the company has access to the personal information of customers or clients. Medical organizations, banks, and law firms are most likely to require signed confidentiality agreements from their employees, but more and more companies see the importance of a formal acknowledgement by employees that they are not free to discuss issues involving customers or clients. This kind of signed agreement should be a part of the employee's personnel file. The HIPAA Health Insurance Portability and Accountability Act of 1996 closely defines how medical establishments must deal with information regarding patients. A company will protect itself to some extent if an employee discusses a patient, and the company can prove the employee agreed to comply with confidentiality. Proprietary information includes product development, new account acquisition efforts, and changes in market focus that would have a negative impact on the company if competition or the general markets were to learn of it.

Housekeeping Issues

Phones, E-Mails, Breaks, Supplies, Parking

The telephone is the heart and soul of many organizations,

so policies regarding its use are ubiquitous. To maintain its corporate image and consistency when dealing with customers and clients, many companies prefer that employees answer all calls in the same, professional manner, such as "Good afternoon, Human Resource Department, Jane Smith. May I be of assistance?" The company may also have a policy about how long a customer or client may be on hold. This may even entail the onerous task of picking up the phone periodically to inform the customer "Please continue to hold — I am still researching your question for you." Often a recorded message has been developed to handle this task.

In addition, most companies have a policy regarding employee use of phones for personal calls. Outside of monitoring employee calls, it is difficult to enforce a "no personal phone calls" policy for employees who are on the phone most of the time for business reasons. Most companies also recognize that, as long as personal phone calls are short and necessary, it is the mark of a compassionate company not to forbid them. An employee may have a child call when he gets home from school, a spouse may remind the employee to pick up milk on the way home, or the employee may call home to say he or she will be late, and no reasonable employer would have a problem with short calls of this nature. The culprits are the ones who spend as much time as they can get away with chatting or conducting personal business on the company phone on company time. How then, to limit unreasonable, indiscriminate use while allowing for those times when a personal call is necessary? Telephone monitoring violates federal wiretap laws, and is therefore illegal unless it is for legitimate business purposes. Recording customer service calls, ostensibly for training purposes, but frequently for problem-resolution purposes is allowable as a legitimate business purpose, and the customer must be told that the call may be recorded.

Monitoring employee phone calls to find out if they are making personal phone calls is not a legitimate business purpose and is against the law. Additionally, it may be considered an invasion of the employee's privacy. Human nature being what it is, most co-workers will be annoyed at a fellow employee who spends his or her working hours on personal phone calls and will complain to a supervisor. Simply having a policy that forbids excessive personal phone calls and enforcing it may be all a company requires.

However, e-mail has become the twenty-first century version of the phone and controlling its use is more difficult than controlling phone use. First of all, the example above of co-workers self-enforcing a personal phone call policy will not work. Fellow employees can overhear phone conversations and realize they are clearly personal, but they may not see the content of e-mails. In addition to sending e-mails and instant messaging, a wide range of activities including shopping, making travel reservations and researching new home prices can take place online, providing unlimited opportunities for abuse. Improper browsing, such as on pornographic sites, can lead to accusations of sexual harassment.

E-mails sent are retrievable, even if they have been deleted. These can be and have been used as documentation in harassment or discrimination cases. Because of this, some companies do use a system of Internet monitoring, access limitation, or a combination of both to prevent abuse of e-mail and the Internet. Because employee e-mails may be used as documents of evidence against a business in court, it is reasonable to limit its use. Most court rulings have not allowed employee invasion-of-privacy claims to stand since the computer, the Internet access system, and documents created on it have been deemed to be possessions of the employer. The first line of defense, however, as in the case with telephone calls, is to have a clear policy in place regarding e-mail or Internet use at the office. An employer should be able to expect that the company Internet will be used only for company business.

The proverbial Monday morning water cooler crowd has long been the subject of comedy routines. "Goofing off," however, does have a real cost to a company. Once again, prudent management will find a middle ground between severely limiting breaks and private conversations among employees and realizing that employee morale involves a certain amount of bonding over such common issues as the news, TV shows, or weekend sporting events. For hourly employees, the law covers some aspects of breaks. If a break is longer than 20 minutes, the employee can be considered off duty and is not eligible to be paid. This is meant to cover lunch periods and the longer midmorning and midafternoon breaks that are typically taken in jobs requiring manual labor. Those 90 minutes are usually calculated as outside of the working day. Some states have meal and rest break requirements, but federal law does not.

Smoking breaks can adversely affect productivity. Now that most buildings are smoke-free, employers have been obligated to allow smokers to go outside or to a designated smoking area for a cigarette. The smokers may be losing time and creating resentment on the part of employees who do not smoke and therefore do not get this additional break time. Unless it has specific break periods written into its policy, which is frequently unreasonable in a small office environment, the company will have to rely on good supervision to monitor abuse. As long as there is no blatant abuse and productivity does not suffer, most companies allow employees to relax once in a while.

Each employee should expect to have the proper supplies on hand, provided by the company, to allow him or her to function properly. Obviously, certain craftspeople and technicians will supply their own tools, but normally, companies consider office, factory, and other supplies as a cost of conducting business. Nevertheless, theft by employees of supplies and services, including copying, faxing, phone calls, and Internet use, can create a financial burden for a company. Some firms resort to such draconian measures as requiring employees to use their own pens and pencils or issuing one set of supplies and requiring employees to supply subsequent replacements. Other companies may appoint a supply administrator who metes out supplies and monitors overuse. In this case as well, the company policy should guide the intent by disallowing personal use of supplies, photocopying, and faxing, with supervisors responsible for enforcing the policy.

Depending on the location of the organization, parking can be a big issue. If a company is located in the downtown business district of a large city, parking will probably not be provided. Companies in the suburbs or in corporate parks are not obligated to supply parking, but it would be difficult for such a company to attract employees (or customers for that matter) without available parking. If a company does supply parking facilities, it is only required to follow laws concerning handicapped parking. Any other restrictions or arrangements are by choice. In some companies the CEO and other top officials get the best spots. In others, all employees park farther away so the customers can have the best spots. The concept of preferential parking for senior management stems from the idea that because their time is valuable, they should not spend it traversing the parking lot. There is always some resentment when VIPs get preferential treatment, so many companies have designated a prime spot for the employee of the month. If you have a policy, make sure it is understood by all and applied systematically.

Do all of these issues require a policy in the personnel handbook? The answer depends on the size of the company and its experience with abuses in each area. Frequently, policies are written or changed to address problems, which is why a personnel handbook has to be a "living" document, updated as needs and times change.

Explanation of the Personnel Handbook

When the personnel handbook or policy is introduced, senior management or the head of the human resource department should have a company-wide orientation (by department, division, or location if the company is large) explaining the salient points of the policy. A record should be kept that each employee attended this orientation, understood the policy, and received a copy, if applicable. Each supervisor who will be responsible for enforcing the policy should receive in-depth training on all of the points of the handbook and be able to explain them to his or her department. Whenever a change is made to the policy, it should be announced in writing and disseminated in such a way that the company can have a record of each employee's acknowledgement and understanding of the change. If a major revision of policy is made, the company should conduct another company-wide training, outlining the changes and retraining supervisors in effectively using the revised policy. When a new employee joins the company, he should receive the most recent version of the employee handbook as part of his orientation. These steps are necessary to ensure that no employees "fall through the cracks" in terms of having the policy explained to them. If the policy is explained only at the initial introduction, new employees will be at a disadvantage. If it is only explained to new employees as they join the company, existing employees will have to rely on their own interpretation of the policy. Following these steps will all ensure that all employees have had the policies explained to them.

Initial Training

Thorough orientation and training will ensure that the employee is able to efficiently and effectively perform the duties of her position. In addition, this orientation and training help to make an employee feel like a valued member of the organization, a proven motivator in positive employee behavior. Acquainting the employee with such basics as the personnel policies, how the phone systems work, where the copy machines are, what normal working hours are, who handles which responsibilities, and so on will save the employee, her supervisor, and many others in the company both time and trouble the first few weeks. Having to learn all of the ins and outs of a company by trial and error will lead to frustration and even error on the part of the new employee and wasted time for everyone else. An employee's, and consequently a company's, performance will suffer if a new employee is not oriented properly.

The orientation should put the new employee at ease and make her feel welcome, give her a basic understanding of the operations of the company and her place in it, and ease her into her new position with as little stress as possible. Using a mentoring program is one way to make this process successful. The new employee will see, as she works her way through learning a new job, that there is someone who can answer her questions when she is confused or uncertain. Typically, orientation of a new employee will be passed from one department to another, especially in the case of a large company. The new employee may have benefits and personnel policy explained to her by the HR department, learn the telephone system from the receptionist, the computer system from the IT department, security and safety procedures from the office manager, the requisition system from the supply manager, and then finally be turned over to her supervisor for training in her own department. This process introduces the new employee to many people in the company, but it is still essential that there is a single person overseeing the entire process and to whom the employee can turn in case she becomes overwhelmed.

After a general, company-wide orientation, the new employee should be put in the capable hands of her supervisor for in-depth training. The length of time for this training depends on many factors. The field of training itself has become a big, complex business. Large companies have entire departments devoted to training, numbers of books have been written about it, and university degrees are offered in training. Suffice it to say that, depending on the complexity of the position, a training period of a few days to a few weeks will be required before a new employee can work independently in a position.

Some jobs are fairly generic, so if the employee has basic training and skills in the job (especially if she was hired because of her previous experience) she should require only an introduction to the company's unique way of doing things. Each position should have a job description and a task list that can be used as guidelines for the training schedule. More often than not, a new employee will learn by sitting down and doing the job, while the supervisor or others in the department correct, oversee, and answer questions. According to Gary Dessler in *Human Resource Management,* the majority, or about two-thirds, of training is this "informal learning." Ideally, the trainer should outline the job, expectations, and performance requirements and then work with the new employee honing his skills to perform at his optimum level. If the supervisor or trainer has developed a detailed job description, the new employee can follow along instead of having to make his own notes, "reinventing the wheel." On a more sophisticated level, if training programs are tied into long-term goals, new competencies can be built into the training programs to allow for smooth transitions to new programs, markets, and products. Superior initial training programs that are tied into long-term development will also allow the company to target inadequacies and develop further training for the future.

Opportunities for Additional Training

Few employees want to stay in the same position and do the same job for the rest of their lives. In order to advance, employees will have to learn new and different skills. One of the goals of performance evaluations should be to target inadequacies so that training can improve current job performance. Evaluations also should be used to identify strengths that will lead to advancement. So whether additional training is offered as a corrective action to improve current performance or as a motivational action to enhance skills for future advancement, evaluation programs are valuable tools. Most companies offer advanced training for targeted employees to assist in retention, to ensure continuity in succession planning, and to improve competitiveness. Training is expensive, however, whether it is done in-house or by outside trainers, both in terms of hard costs (real dollars) and in terms of time.

Companies need to assess the cost-benefit ratios of any training programs. This assessment is not easy, however, and companies will use different methods to evaluate whether a real benefit is derived. Evaluation forms assess whether the employee believes the training improved his skills or prepared him for additional or different duties. Exams attempt to measure what or how much the employee learned through the training. Impact studies are designed to learn whether the additional training did what it intended to do: increased sales, improved customer service, decreased response time. The overall intent is to determine if the training actually benefited the company more than it cost the company.

Career Development Plans

Even though most employee development takes the form of on-the-job training, often a company will identify individuals they recognize will form the basis of future senior management and develop a specific plan with this in mind. In many instances, a senior mentor relationship (also known as the coach-understudy approach) will be established so that the employee can shadow a senior person and observe, question, and learn from him or her. Individuals in a career development plan, whether it is formally recognized as such, will be encouraged to seek out seminars and courses as well as to observe operations in their own and other departments.

If a person is recognized to have senior management potential, he may be assigned rotating schedules in different departments to learn more about the general company, outside of his own sphere of expertise. Many times employees who have been singled out as management material will be offered the opportunity for advanced education, such as an MBA, at the company's expense. Such concepts of leadership training tend to be more organizationally developed than in the past. In other words, the company seeks a concrete benefit to itself in addition to the benefit to the employee. Many times a company that offers this type of program will require a commitment from the employee in the form of a contract or guaranteed term with a buyout clause reimbursing a portion of the educational expense.

Security Systems and Procedures

In the not too distant past, the only businesses that needed complex security measures were banks. Companies would lock up at night to prevent burglaries, and perhaps some had night security personnel, but for the most part, companies felt comfortable that the presence of staff would deter unauthorized access. Today most companies have some measure of security in place, at least to protect their staff from outside dangers. Increased security measures help protect employees and should be considered standard for most companies. Standard security includes adequate lighting, especially in such areas as halls, stairwells, and parking lots; mounted mirrors to view around corners; keys or codes for admission to buildings; silent alarms connected both to the police and to a security company; and surveillance cameras. If a company routinely deals with cash, additional precautions should be taken. Drop boxes and lock boxes should be used; staff handling cash should not be alone. All staff, especially security staff, should be trained in conflict resolution and nonviolent responses. Do not expect or encourage staff to risk their lives to save company assets.

The effectiveness of these measures will be severely reduced if employees are not trained in proper security. A portion of new employee orientation should be devoted to using proper security measures in and around the job site. Employees should be trained to be alert for suspicious-acting persons in the parking lot and in approaches to the building. Employees should pay attention to the mirrors and surveillance TVs if visible. It is not just in comedy movies that a crime is occurring in full view of a surveillance camera while unsuspecting employees are busy doing something else. All staff should be forbidden to make copies of keys or give out key codes to anyone. An inventory should be kept of keys that have been distributed, and only the responsible party in the security department should be allowed to make copies of keys. Any employees who are responsible for opening or closing the building should be trained to disarm the alarm system out of view of unauthorized persons. A procedure should be developed to evacuate the building safely in case of violent attack.

Modern violence has taken so many different forms that some companies have resorted to opening mail with tools and gloved hands and to accepting only packages with return address labels.

Even the fairly common procedure of terminating an employee requires stringent security measures. Good sense dictates that the terminated employee be required to return keys and any other company property, especially laptop computers and portable phones. Any company that issues such office equipment as this should keep an inventory of any items that have been issued. In addition, to protect vital information, a company must change passwords when an employee leaves. To further inhibit access to the company grounds, departing employees must surrender any badges or identification that allows access. Terminating an employee has, in recent years, also meant that a company needed to be on alert for retaliation. Sufficient security measures should be in place at all times, but security staff should be informed whenever a controversial dismissal has taken place.

Use of Company Vehicles

A valuable perk that some companies afford certain employees is the use of company cars. Current prices of vehicles, auto insurance, and fuel make this benefit immensely appealing to any employee who is eligible. Some government organizations have severely cut back on this benefit for public employees because of outcry about the costs to taxpayers. Private industry, however, is free to continue to supply this benefit. Usually, the staff who use company cars are on the road most of the day for the company. Companies restrict the use of company cars for any number of reasons. Insurance coverage may only extend the time the vehicle is in use for company business or en route, thereby requiring the employee to keep a log of miles. The vehicle may have to stay on company property on weekends, necessitating alternate commuting methods for the employee. However, some companies provide a company vehicle with few or no restrictions to senior employees. This is considered a part of the total compensation package, usually negotiated when the executive joins the company.

Ken Patterson Sr.
ASM/EMT/PSM/CSSO

Our company employs 2,500 employees, and we have a very detailed written personnel policy. Most of our employees, I'd say more than 85 percent, know whom to contact if they have problems, questions, or concerns.

Each position in the company has an accompanying written job description, which is essential, particularly when we are hiring. We generally use Job Services to recruit qualified candidates for open positions. To determine which applicants will be offered an interview, HR reviews candidates to find those who closely match the requirements of the position, and then the manager/director of the area conducts the interviews.

During the application process, testing is dependent on the open job. However, for all positions, we ask applicants to tell us their goals in five years, why they want to work with us, and why they left their last position. That tells us a lot about applicants. Alternately, the most important concern for most applicants is our health insurance and tuition reimbursement.

We require secret clearances, so a very thorough background check is conducted on all new employees, and employees are made aware that we do perform drug and alcohol testing. At minimum, all new employees undergo one week of orientation and then there's on-the-job training as the job requires.

CHAPTER 8

Communicating with Employees

The term "team" has become the tag word of corporate discussion and literature. Building a corporate team has become the goal of most forward-thinking company executives, since this implies that all of the members of the company (team) recognize that they have a common goal, for the company to succeed (win), and every employee (team member) works toward that goal together. The only way a sports team, the analogy upon which this concept is built, succeeds is by excellent communication. Communication among managers, coaches, and the rest of the players is imperative if a team is to succeed. In successful, dynamic organizations, communication is constant and flows freely both up and down the organization. Gone are the days when the boss would pronounce a directive and the employees unquestioningly followed it. Today's work environment is comprised of focus groups, empowerment initiatives, and interactive teams, and management is intent not only on listening to but also using the input from these groups. Today's companies are more and more likely to appeal to the rank-and-file to assist management in developing solutions to the company's problems.

Not informing employees about corporate goals and results and not listening to feedback from those on the front lines have been proven to have serious negative consequences. Companies use many methods to ensure that good communication, in and of itself, is treated as a common goal.

Establishing "Official Communications"

Establishing a goal of two-way communication does not mean that a company will rely on informal methods to let the employees know what is going on in the company. One of the most important aspects of good communication is the clarity mentioned above, and one way to achieve it is to make sure employees can "separate the wheat from the chaff." If employees believe that the company communicates effectively, they do not have to second-guess what is happening within the company. When companies are reticent about sharing information, the rumor mill goes into high gear. Ironically, these rumors are usually more devastating than the truth that the company may have been hiding. When a company freely shares information, both positive and negative, with its employees, there is no grist for the rumor mill. Members of the staff are confident that they know the whole picture. How does a company make sure that the information its employees receives is accurate? All too often, the biggest culprits in disseminating false information are middle managers, who believe they have to act as though they know what is going on and just make up something. Keep management informed and involved, and encourage them to keep their staff informed about developments. Make sure that the management team is as open about communication as the company is. Open meetings by senior management as well as written notices of decisions taken or new directions being considered will help employees realize that they are getting firsthand information. Of course, some insider information has to be restricted if it can be construed to affect the future performance of the company's stock. The company's lawyers should advise in these situations.

One of the most difficult types of information to control concerns works in progress. Many times teams may be developing new policies or products, but they are discouraged from discussing them. Rather than allow partial or misinformation to leak out, why not publish the notes from each meeting and let employees be informed as the project changes and unfolds? Each employee will have an official version and not have to rely on rumors. The advent of e-mail has made distributing information easy and reliable. The informality of it also lends itself to the idea that decisions are not final, that more information is to follow.

Soliciting Employee Feedback

To ensure that a plan of communication takes hold in an organization, you must solicit employee feedback. The tried-and-true suggestion box does work, as long as the company responds to the suggestions. Mentioning them in a newsletter or giving awards for suggestions used are two ways employees know their suggestions have been read. Employee surveys are becoming a popular way for senior management to get the pulse of the organization. Just as with suggestion boxes, however, if the information from the survey is ignored, its usefulness is lost, and it may even create negative feelings among employees. Make sure that whatever information that is solicited from employees is understood and treated with respect; be certain that managers are properly trained in good communication skills.

The best way to solicit employee feedback, however, is the simplest and most logical: by asking. "Management by walking around" was considered a novel concept some years ago when many bosses remained in their offices all day. Now the best top managers are seen on factory floors and in the branch offices talking to employees and asking them how things are going. Of course, this approach works only if management truly involves employees and openly welcomes their comments and suggestions.

Many companies today have CEO meetings in which the president of the company sits with groups of employees or full departments and asks about their concerns and ideas. Some companies have initiated company hot lines that allow employees to express concerns or complaints anonymously. The HR department is charged with resolving or, at least, addressing them.

The bottom line is that if employees know that information they receive comes from a reliable source, they will believe they are treated with respect. Information delivered in this way will be less subject to distortions and will be true to the original intent. If they receive enough information in this manner and are confident that most important information about the company is communicated to them, employees will be better informed and be able to ignore rumors and scuttlebutt that only serve to undermine employee morale.

Good Communication Skills for Managers

One of the most important skills for managers is communication. In fact, most management skills stem from communication skills. How are employees motivated? By communicating goals and objectives to them. How are directives and instructions given? By communicating them. How does a manager help an employee reach his or her full potential? By communicating new lessons and skills. If a person is not a good communicator, he or she will never be able to be a good manager. It must be remembered that communication is a two-way street, and successful managers are adept at soliciting and understanding staff communication. However, most managers think they are better communicators than they actually are, and a company that is committed to good communication should make sure its managers are properly trained in communications skills.

According to Gary Dressler in Human Resource Management, the most important aspects of communication are engagement, explanation, and expectation. One must engage the listener and make sure that ideas transmitted are at least understood, if not necessarily accepted. At the same time, the communicator must engage himself so that any feedback and comments can be heard, understood, and incorporated. A good communicator will be knowledgeable about his subject so that he can easily explain concepts and be able to elaborate if further clarification is needed. An expectation should be built into any business communication so that all the parties are clear about what should result from the conversation. The result may not fulfill the expectation that either party had at the outset, given compromises and adjustments resulting from good communication, but there should be a satisfactory outcome or result, indicating that all parties understand and agree on actions to be taken.

Every company should make good communication an

essential part of the management training. Managers should be trained not only to use positive, proactive language, but also to speak clearly and precisely, avoiding annoying speech habits like monotone voices or such verbal crutches as "uh," "ya know," "right," and "okay." Managers should be trained to deliver messages with tact and empathy and to "praise in public, correct in private." Many untrained managers are happy to point out every error a worker makes and never congratulate him for a job well done. Body language is another essential component of language. Delivering good news with a frown or trying to be open and encouraging with an employee while one's arms are firmly crossed against the chest sends mixed signals, undermining the intended message. A manager must discipline himself so that his own emotional state does not influence the delivery of the message. Most importantly managers should be reminded to listen. Frequently, communications trainers advise students to restate the audience's response so that both are clear that the message communicated is the message intended. The importance of good, clear communication cannot be emphasized enough, and a company that makes sure its management team is sending the right messages, in the right way, will have an advantage in business.

Conducting Meetings

Meetings are usually one of the primary ways in which decisions are made and communicated to staff. Why then, do most people consider meetings a waste of time?

Meetings need to be organized to be productive. All too often, meetings start late and run over, or meeting attendees are allowed to discuss tangent topics unrelated to the business at hand, and, as a result, no conclusions, solutions, or future actions are determined. A meeting like this truly is a waste of time. Nothing is more frustrating than sitting through a two-hour meeting and realizing that no decision was made as a result of it.

To be effective, meetings must:

- Be small.

- Have an agenda that is followed.

- Involve all attendees.

- End on time.

- Have meeting notes with "decisions taken" and "follow-up actions" (and the persons responsible for those actions) noted.

Keeping a meeting small adds to its effectiveness for a number of reasons. First, not much business can be conducted if too many people have a say in the matter. Inviting people to the meeting who are not involved in the process, who have no interest in the subject at hand, or who have no authority in the matter will prolong the meeting with no concrete benefits. Limit the attendees of your meetings to those who have a real stake in the outcome, and to those who can act on the decisions made at the meeting. An exception, of course, is a meeting that is purely for the purpose of disseminating information. A meeting to introduce the new employee handbook, for example, may well be a company-wide meeting attended by most of the employees. Even in this case, a better solution would be to introduce the handbook in smaller department or division meetings. Another possibility is to follow up the corporate-wide meeting with question-and-answer meetings held by department managers or supervisors who have been further trained. Small group meetings will encourage employees to ask questions.

Write an agenda and follow it. It is frustrating to go to a meeting with the expectation that an issue will be addressed or resolved, only to have most of the meeting devoted to something else. The person who is running the meeting should set the agenda and time. Make sure to keep the agenda limited to a few issues, allowing enough time for each. No meeting should last more than two hours, or the meeting will fall apart at the end. Be courteous but firm if anyone strays off topic or digs up old dirt that will not serve the meeting's purpose. The meeting should be purposeful, not an arena for people to find fault or gripe. Stick to the topics on the agenda and move through them in an orderly fashion. Logically, if you have five topics for a one-hour meeting, each topic should be allotted 12 minutes. Begin wrap-up discussion on each topic after ten minutes. If some topics are more complex or pressing, consider putting those issues at the beginning of the meeting and allowing more time for them. Having an agenda will force participants to be organized. Handouts, slides, or other presentation and informational items will have to be arranged or distributed beforehand to stay within time limits.

If only people who are interested and involved in the topics will be invited to the meeting, each attendee should participate. If a discussion is progressing without input from one of the attendees, be the one to ask "What's your take on this?" However, avoid letting one of the meeting attendees take over the whole discussion; if this happens, it is no longer a meeting. It is a speech.

Once the time is set for a meeting, it is imperative to stick to it. First, most people attending will have planned their business day around the ending time of the meeting and will have to leave; if the meeting continues after people have left, vital input will be missed. Second, ending on time will help you follow the agenda.

Taking notes and assigning responsibilities are two of the most crucial aspects of a meeting. It is a sad fact of business that many hours are spent in meetings in which great ideas are generated and solutions are presented and then nothing happens. If no one was charged with keeping track of the ideas and solutions, and if no one was assigned the tasks of implementing them, then they will slide into oblivion. If anything is decided, make sure some action is assigned to move it along to completion. Minutes of the meeting and the actions decided upon should be distributed to all who attended, as well as to anyone who may be affected by outcomes.

Open-Door Policy

When employees believe that senior management is accessible, they are apt to work harder for the company's success. One of the most successful companies in the United States, Costco, which is, according to Wikepedia.com, the first company ever to grow from zero to three billion dollars in sales in less than six years, is famous for the "management by walking around" style of its corporate founder, James Sinegal who wears a "CAN I HELP YOU?" badge when he visits the stores. His fellow employees are comfortable talking to him about both concerns and suggestions. His opinion is that the best place to find out how to run a company is right on the floor with the people who are selling your products and meeting your customers day in and day out.

Companies that encourage management to be accessible to employees give themselves an important advantage in employee relationships. As with most policies, accessibility must be implemented from the top down and practiced, not just preached. If the head of the company is only seen at board meetings and shareholder meetings but says that he has an open-door policy, senior and middle management will assume they, too, have the right to "talk the talk" without "walking the walk." Granted, the CEO of a large company will not have the time to meet with every employee with a problem, but solutions such as CEO meetings or random, casual visits to the factory floor or regional offices will convey the message to management and to rank-and-file employees that direct contact and input from every employee is welcomed and encouraged.

How is this culture attained? Meetings and contacts will keep the idea in the mind of each employee. Just as a CEO will meet with his senior staff on a weekly or even daily basis, that senior staff should relay the ideas communicated via their meetings with middle managers, middle managers to department managers, department managers to supervisors, and all the way on down. A quick meeting on the factory floor to learn what was discussed yesterday at the CEO's weekly roundtable will work wonders in making employees feel part of the organization. Managers on each level should be encouraged to allow employees to come to them with problems and concerns. A top-down philosophy will work to control how this is done. Each employee should be encouraged to bring his concerns to his "first line of defense." A worker should be able to talk easily to his line supervisor, the line supervisor to his department head, the department head to the division head, and so on all the way to the president. An open-door policy does not dismiss an orderly system of hierarchy; responsibilities have to be described and addressed on each level. However, if employees at each level of responsibility are allowed and encouraged to bring their concerns forward, each employee will be empowered within the organization, believing that his voice is heard.

CHAPTER 9

Evaluating and Motivating Performance

Appraising employee performance is a crucial element of managing. The appraisal process assists employees in understanding their duties and responsibilities and lets them know if they have been meeting expectations. The appraisal process can also be used to identify additional training that will improve employee performance. Most organizations use a formal appraisal process in which standards are set and judged based on pre-determined criteria. In other words, the performance of duties in a job description is measured routinely and this measurement becomes the basis for raises or advancement. Most supervisors dislike the appraisal process because they view it as an obligation to find faults in an employee's performance, putting them both in an adversarial position. Many companies have abandoned the formal appraisal process and replaced it with a more frequent, informal feedback system in which the supervisor outlines expectations, and the employee outlines what he or she needs to meet those expectations. The benefits of a well-structured and properly administered appraisal system cannot be underestimated, and taking the time and trouble to implement one will reap rewards well beyond the efforts invested.

The Appraisal Process

An employee must know what is expected of him. In most cases, companies use the appraisal or performance review process to communicate weaknesses in performance and recommend solutions to correct those weaknesses; to identify strengths in performance and capitalize on those strengths; and to determine compensation, bonuses, and advancement based on the measured performance. Properly administered, an appraisal program will also serve to enhance many of the employee-management initiatives in which the company and its managers are routinely engaged. It will create a forum to focus on under-performing employees.

Many supervisors will avoid confrontation with an employee who is not working up to par until the situation becomes untenable and the employee has to be let go. Interim discussions regarding performance could prevent such situations as the periodic review will force the issue to be raised. In turn, perhaps employee and supervisor will achieve a meeting of the minds. Performance appraisals motivate employees to improve their skills and knowledge and to examine their career goals. Appraisals reinforce employees' understanding of the company's and the department's goals and values. A model appraisal process will aid the company's training by targeting needs or determining new training needs that have to be addressed. Lastly, a good appraisal system will form a concrete, legal basis for most of the key human resource decisions that a company has to make in terms of hiring, firing, compensation, and promotion. Of course, it will be carefully designed to avoid any taint of discrimination.

In addition to outlining duties to be performed by designing job descriptions, the company should set performance standards, or benchmarks, that allow employees to know whether they are performing adequately or superbly. These benchmarks should be developed along with the job description and should be observable and measurable and able to be documented. The complexity of the job will determine the standards used. A routine job can have fixed standards like quantity produced per hour or per day, with a quality control level incorporated to ensure that quality is not sacrificed for quantity. When a job is more complex, however, quantitative measurements are difficult to apply.

Normally, in management or creative jobs, evaluations are made on a results basis. Specific procedures should be defined and used to track behavior and monitor performance. Most standards are established through the experience of previous jobholders. If the average number of entries that a data-entry clerk makes in an hour is 500, then 400 may be considered acceptable, and 700 outstanding. If 95 percent accuracy is the average, 90 percent may be acceptable and 100 percent considered outstanding. Standards like these should be as specific and as measurable as possible. They also need to be attainable. If a top data-entry clerk can enter 700 items per hour with 99 percent accuracy, that level cannot be set as the benchmark. It certainly can be set as a standard goal, with meeting the goal consistently representing the top rating in that area of performance. These performance standards and goals should be outlined clearly to employees. It is unfair to inform an employee at her three-month appraisal meeting that she has been entering only 300 items per hour when the expectation is 500. The employee needs a standard by which to measure her work as well as a goal to work toward.

Types of Performance Appraisals

Even though all appraisal systems are designed to establish a methodical way to evaluate employee performance, there are different ways to approach this goal. Sessions may be formal or informal, and different rating systems may be used. The system used will depend on the level of the employees evaluated and on how much of the company's resources will be devoted to the system. Supervisors or other evaluators must be adequately trained in the measurement procedures to ensure fairness to all.

Modern thinking in this area has demonstrated that establishing standards by which an employee can measure himself and setting goals to work toward are the most successful types of appraisals. This is the basis for the most widely used appraisal method, Management by Objective, or MBO (*Human Resource Management*, 9th Edition, Gary Dessler). The manager and employee should meet at the beginning of the appraisal period to discuss their mutual goals for the employee's job performance. These goals should encompass the organization's goals and the department's goals as well as the employee's individual goals. The key that is critical is that these goals need to be established *before* the period of performance. In other systems, the performance appraisal has become a kind of "gotcha!" in which the employee is informed about ways he was not performing to standards. Clearly this is unfair if the standards were not spelled out in the beginning. MBO appraisals seek to set clear, specific, measurable goals that the employee accepts and agrees to work toward. If goals are arbitrary and the employee deems them unattainable, the process will suffer. Both the supervisor and the employee must have a clear idea of the job and its standards and limitations. MBO appraisals have an advantage over other types of appraisals because of the way employees are involved in the process, identifying skills to be measured and goals to be set.

Employee input is critical to the success of the system.

Employees no longer expect to receive a report written by their supervisor in which they are informed of the weaknesses of their performance and the requirements for improvement. MBO also avoids the phenomenon in which a supervisor remembers only the most recent incidents in an employee's performance and uses those as the basis for the appraisal. Because the employee is integral to the evaluation, he can counter with incidents that balance any weaknesses in recent performance to draw an overall picture. The supervisor should make sure that whatever observations he has made can be substantiated by fact and observation. A supervisor may be evaluating 20 employees and draws on recent memory for each one, while an employee has to think only about his or her own performance. MBO on the other hand, pits the employee against only himself: he helps to set his goals and works in conjunction with his supervisor to find ways to meet them.

Max Messmer lists some less frequently used and subjective appraisal systems in *Human Resources for Dummies*:

- Essay appraisals, in which the supervisor is asked to write statements describing the employee's performance in listed areas.

- Critical-incidents reporting, in which the evaluator keeps a log of incidents reflecting specific examples of good or bad performances.

- Job rating checklist, in which a form is used to check off or rate statements of performance.

- Behaviorally Anchored Rating Scale (BARS), in which the behaviors, traits, or skills to perform a job function are rated on a bar scale.

- Forced choice appraisals, in which the evaluator chooses a statement or rank that applies to the employee's performance, as in "always does this task well" or "never does this task well."

- Ranking methods of appraisals, in which all employees are ranked on a best to worst scale.

Other appraisal methods involve evaluations by one's peers, by one's subordinates, or by a rating committee. Another is to use a self-rating system that is compared to the rating by the supervisor or other evaluator.

Research in this area will yield a number of alternate systems of appraisals, as well as boilerplate forms that can be used to administer them. Deciding which one to use depends on the budget and length of time to devote to appraisals. Whatever system is used, the most important factor in its success will be that it has the support of all involved. Senior management must agree with the process and the system chosen to implement it, and employees must believe that the system is fair and will achieve the end it intends — improved performance through feedback and training. For this to happen, employees must view the measurements used as fair and directly related to job performance, and they must view the methods for observing and judging job performance as accurate.

Schedules for Appraisals

Most companies perform appraisals on a fixed cycle, with cycles shorter at the beginning of employment and moving to a company-wide standard for all employees. The usual cycles are quarterly for new employees and then annually after their first anniversary. New hires need early and frequent feedback on their performance. Because they have not yet fully absorbed the corporate culture, they may not even know their performance is sub-par if not reviewed frequently.

Appointments for appraisals should be scheduled well in advance, at least a week; employees should not be caught off guard, and they should have time to prepare if they feel it is necessary. The appointment should be confirmed by both parties, not dictated by the supervisor. Adequate time should be allotted for the interview, but it should not be allowed to drag on because an open-ended interview can become a contest of who can talk longest in defense of his or her position. Appraisals should be held in a private, quiet atmosphere without interruption. If the person administering the appraisal does not have a private office, the company should make one available for the purpose of these interviews.

Conducting the Appraisal Interview

Who should be responsible for the overall appraisal process and the appraisal interview? Does it necessarily have to be the same person? The employee's supervisor is most likely the best person to observe and evaluate an employee's performance, but new methods of appraisals, as discussed above, may warrant administration by some other party, perhaps someone from the HR staff.

Regardless of who conducts the appraisal interview, one of the most important determinants of its success or failure is the way in which it is opened. The appraiser outlines the goals of the interview and the appraisal; defines how the employee and the company will benefit from it; explains (especially to new employees) how the criteria have been developed, measured, and applied; explains what the results of the appraisal will be used for (for example, raises, promotions, developing training needs); and lists what rights the employee has if he disagrees with the appraisal. The appraiser should clarify that the interview is expected to be a two-way conversation, and the employee is encouraged to comment on any of the supervisor's remarks. The most comfortable way to establish this rapport is to ask the employee how *he* feels things have been going in his job and career.

The appraiser already has the ultimate result of the appraisal at hand, and should therefore be aware of any potential problems that may arise, including defensiveness on the part of the employee or even hostility to the process. The appraiser must avoid personal bias and conduct the interview in an objective manner, even if the employee is difficult. The appraiser should have a plan for the end results of the interview: will a correction plan or a development plan to work toward promotion goals have to be put in place, or will the status quo be maintained? Any data that is necessary to the appraisal should be available before the interview starts. The job description, standards used for evaluation, and previous appraisals should be reviewed beforehand and available for reference. The supervisor or other appraiser should also review the employee's file to see if any specific issues have been addressed over the review period, or if the employee has had additional training, special recognition, and so on that may influence the conversation.

The evaluator should attempt to establish a relaxed and friendly atmosphere for the interview but be direct and specific about the performance of the employee. The goal is to make sure the employee leaves with a clear idea of what is expected of him in the future. The tone of the interview should be upbeat and positive. The positive aspects of an employee's performance should be discussed first (and a well-designed appraisal form will be organized in this manner) and the appraiser should stress any improvements that can be made, rather than what mistakes were made. Only objective terms for targets should be used, not personal affronts, such as "You never do as many entries as the rest of the department," but rather "The goal for this task is 500 entries per hour, and your level is currently at 450." Solicit information and input from the employee. Ask the employee for specifics to help him improve. The interviewer should not shy away from the task at hand — poor performance has to be discussed to be corrected, and even if the supervisor does not like to be the bad guy, he needs to recognize the situation and face it. As long as a tactful and objective approach about correcting problems is used, an employee should be able to accept the truth.

However, as mentioned above, be prepared for defensiveness; it is perfectly normal for anyone to defend his behavior or performance. If your critique is objective and you use measurable standards to appraise, you should be able to defuse an uncomfortable situation. A calm demeanor toward an agitated employee may calm things. In any event, give the employee some time to vent his feelings; allowing the employee to calm down will often permit the interviewer to continue. If, however, an interviewer feels the situation is getting out of control, he should leave the room and get help.

If measures need to be taken to improve performance, they can be presented in such a way that the employee feels he is involved in designing these measures and thereby maintain his dignity. However, expectations of improvement should be clear and have a defined time frame within which to be met. Any negative feedback should be carefully worded to avoid the appearance of personal attack, while the appraiser strives to be honest and candid about the issue at hand. Employees should not feel threatened during the appraisal interview, but rather should be made to feel that they are contributing to it and to the results that will arise from it. Perhaps the employee could be asked to summarize the discussion from his viewpoint, so that the supervisor is sure that he understands both the negative and positive aspects of the interview. The employee's opinion of his on-the-job performance may be amazing. A good employee may feel that his performance is inadequate, while a slacker may believe that he is the star of the department. These insights are an invaluable tool for employee management.

The interview should end on a positive note, but the interviewer must make sure the interview ends with the goals and means to achieve those goals clearly defined in a document. Both the supervisor and the employee should sign it. Many companies allow the employee to have a copy, and that is the preferred approach. Some companies require that appraisals be reviewed by a department head so that related actions (raises, bonuses, and so on) will be implemented depending on the rating of the appraisal. The evaluation should then be sent to the HR department and retained in the employee's personnel file.

Moving Forward

After an appraisal interview, the supervisor should establish an action list for any decisions that were made. If a time frame for improvement in certain areas was established, that should be noted. If specific trainings were targeted, the supervisor should schedule them. Be sure that the employee understood that further action is intended. This applies whether the goal was to improve performance or to work toward promotion. Avoid allowing an employee with promotion potential to fall through the cracks. Follow up on training needs to prepare him for the future.

Once a performance improvement goal has been established, both the supervisor and the employee should become partners in seeing that the goal is met. Determine what the final goal is and whether it can or should be met in incremental steps. For example, "Increase entries per hour by ten in each of the next five weeks." Establish which tools or training is necessary to complete the goal, for instance, "Enroll in a keyboarding class within the next three days." Measure performance each week to see if the targets are being met, obtain documentation that the class has been scheduled, and so on. One of the biggest weaknesses in most appraisal programs is that after the interview, everybody goes back to "business as usual," and no benefit is derived from this intensive exercise in human angst. If the appraisal has established steps that need to be taken, either to improve an employee's performance or to move him to the next level of performance, make sure you follow through. Many times a supervisor will have to obtain approval or financing for additional training, but the steps have to be taken to get to that next level. A motivated employee will find out about the additional training, but it is ultimately the responsibility of the supervisor to maintain the quality of his staff. A good manager, supervisor, or department head will keep the training and development department involved to strengthen his department.

CHAPTER 10

Discrimination and Fair Treatment

Discrimination is one of the most sensitive and pervasive issues in the HR field today. Few managers, supervisors, or HR experts are purposefully or openly discriminatory, but all companies must make every effort not to project an appearance of discrimination. From the first contact that a company has with a potential employee, it is important that all staff be trained not to show prejudice in hiring or keeping employees. From the outset, using any criteria other than ability to perform a job is going to be considered discriminatory and should be avoided in all employment practices.

Before hiring someone, be sensitive to the implications of discrimination. Interview questions that delve into any aspect of a person's life that is not directly related to the performance of the job applied for could easily be construed as discriminatory. Companies may not ask the race, religion, national origin, sexual orientation, or physical or mental disability of an applicant. A company should make sure that its staff that is responsible for interviewing candidates is well trained in the right kind of questions. In a nutshell, any question that is not directly related to the performance of the job should not be asked. If the position requires the ability to speak a foreign language, or if this ability would make the candidate more qualified for the position, it can be asked. If there is no legitimate, job-related reason for a question, do not ask it.

Pre-employment tests must be validated to be free of questions that may be favorable to one group or unfavorable to a protected group. Job descriptions also should avoid any reference to race, religion, national origin, sexual orientation, or physical or mental disability. Rarely, an employer can specify a requirement in a job description that may normally be considered discriminatory as long as it is a bona fide occupational qualification, or BFOQ. Females working in a female-residence setting, or certain strength requirements, for example, may be allowed. But even the determination of what is a BFOQ is subject to interpretation. A company may determine that they need someone to drive a forklift. If the job also requires lifting heavy items off the forklift, the company is justified in having a weight-lifting requirement for the job. The implications and interpretations are so subtle that the only way to avoid problems is to focus only on the ability to do the job in question.

The company's employee handbook should contain an equal employment opportunity policy, stating the company is committed to providing equal opportunity to all regardless of race, religion, national origin, sexual orientation, or physical or mental disability. The policy should also contain an anti-harassment policy prohibiting any harassment based on race, religion, national origin, sexual orientation, or physical or mental disability, and an ADA (Americans with Disabilities Act) policy.

Companies should be especially sensitive to the wording of their employment ads to avoid discriminatory language. Such expressions such as "Girl Friday," "handyman," "able-bodied," and "recent college graduate" denote preference of a certain group of people and discriminate against those not falling within those groups.

Even if a company does not openly or knowingly practice discrimination, it can still be found guilty of discrimination if supervisors or workers were engaged in discriminatory behavior and the company did nothing to stop it. This particularly applies in the appraisal process, where promotions, discharges, and merit increases are based on the determination of the supervisor writing the appraisal.

Remember, discrimination is prohibited in all areas of employment, from recruitment and hiring to compensation, benefits, job assignments, employee classifications, transfers, promotions, layoffs, testing, and availability of facilities.

The Laws Governing Discrimination

Many federal, state, and local laws disallow discrimination on the basis of race, religion, sex, age, disability, veteran status, or marital status. A number of states also prohibit discrimination on the basis of sexual orientation. The Equal Employment Opportunity Commission (EEOC) enforces the laws related to discrimination on a federal level. One of the basic requirements every employer should meet is to post the EEOC requirement notices in the place of business to inform employees of their rights under discrimination laws. If the company is large enough, it may be required to file a report with the EEOC that gives them the breakdown of its workforce by discriminated category.

The Americans with Disabilities Act

If a company has 15 or more employees, it is subject to the Americans with Disabilities Act. The ADA makes it illegal to discriminate against employees with disabilities when making hiring and job assignment decisions and also in the treatment of these employees. Employers subject to the provisions of the ADA are also required to make "reasonable" accommodations to enable a person with a disability to perform the duties of a job.

These accommodations range from wheelchair ramps to equipment for vision- or hearing-impaired individuals. These accommodations are required unless the company can prove that providing them will prove an undue hardship. "Undue hardship" is usually defined in financial terms, so that a smaller company that has to build ramps or buy special equipment may be excused, while a larger, more successful company would not. Citing financial hardship is no excuse not to hire people with disabilities. Many times, reasonable accommodations can be made with little or no expense to the company. One medical office hired an individual for the billing department, which was located on the second floor, but, in order to accommodate her, connected a computer to the system for her on the first floor. It turned out to be a better solution because she was next to the front desk and could easily help with frequent billing questions. Adhering to ADA regulations has frequently turned out not only to be the right thing to do, but the better thing to do in terms of good corporate policy.

Age Discrimination in Employment Act

The Age Discrimination in Employment Act (ADEA) of 1967 prohibits discrimination against individuals aged 40 or older. It applies to any organization with 20 or more employees. This law states that a company may not refuse to hire someone who is 40 or older as long as he or she is able to perform the duties of the position. It also prohibits mandatory retirement at any age, with one exception: a company may require a senior executive to retire at a certain age. Most applications do not ask a person's age, but if a company is trying to avoid hiring older employees, a person's general age is no secret. Those companies may be eliminating some of the most experienced candidates by discriminatory against older potential employees.

Title VII of the Civil Rights Act of 1964

An employer may not refuse employment because of race, color, religion, sex, or national origin as mandated by Title VII. A number of court decisions have also held that this act prohibits discrimination on the basis of sexual preference. The law applies to employers with 15 or more employees, but most states have adopted civil rights laws of their own and applied them more stringently to companies with as few as one employee (namely Alaska, Colorado, Hawaii, Iowa, Maine, Michigan, and Minnesota). Many states had fair employment acts older than Title VII, but Title VII is recognized as the most important law regarding discrimination, and most employers have made efforts to comply.

Larger companies have, of late, added equal employment officers to their HR staff, and smaller companies have made sure that some member of the management team is responsible for the effort. Today it seems unreasonable to imagine that in the early part of the 20th century, companies could still advertise for "Protestants Only." Today a company can be required to accommodate a person's religious practices as long as it does not result in an undue hardship to the company. An example would be to allow a Muslim employee to go to a place in the building where he could pray. Title VII has also succeeded in erasing some of the stereotypes in gender hiring. Many jobs, including carpentry, plumbing, engineering, and accounting were considered men's jobs, and others, such as teaching, nursing, and secretarial work were considered exclusively women's. Today, the lines are much more blurred.

The Equal Pay Act

The Equal Pay Act requires equal pay for substantially equal work; that is, work requiring equivalent skills, effort, and responsibilities that is done under substantially the same circumstances whether performed by a man or a woman. For the purposes of this act, fringe benefits are considered pay, so a man cannot receive a different level of benefits than a woman who has the same job. Many companies have withheld raises for women contending that they have to be home with children more often and can't travel or work overtime, while this idea may have nothing to do with reality.

Vietnam Era Veterans' Readjustment Assistance Act

The Vietnam Era Veterans' Readjustment Assistance Act calls for employers with government contracts of more than $10,000 to take affirmative action to hire disabled veterans of the Vietnam era.

Vocational Rehabilitation Act of 1973

This act requires employers with federal contracts of more than $2,500 to use affirmative action techniques to ensure that people with disabilities are hired.

Adverse Impact and Disparate Treatment

Adverse impact occurs when the effect of a company policy, even if it is nondiscriminatory on its face, affects a protected group more than others. These instances frequently evolve when long-standing practices are not adjusted to meet the reality of today's laws. One of the most famous cases involved a an Afro-American Domino's Pizza employee who was prohibited from wearing a beard because of company policy. The courts found that the policy discriminated against Afro-Americans because of a common skin disorder (pseudofolliculitis barbae) suffered by more than half of the Afro-American male population that prevents them from shaving. This policy of Domino's had an adverse impact on Afro-Americans, many of whom would not be able to work for Domino's because of this condition. (*Bradley v. Pizzaco of Nebraska dba Domino's Pizza, U.S. Court of Appeals, 8th Circuit, No. 89-2271NE, 1991.*)

Disparate treatment primarily deals with testing of potential candidates for employment. If more of one particular group consistently fails to pass employment qualification exams, the exam may be considered discriminatory by the EEOC which has formulated a test to determine failure rates that should be considered disparate. A selection rate for any racial, ethnic, or sex group that is less than four-fifths or 80 percent of the rate for the group with the highest rate will generally be regarded as evidence of adverse impact, while a greater than four-fifths rate will generally not be regarded as evidence of adverse impact. In other words, if more than 80 percent of your male applicants are hired on the basis of your tests, and only 20 percent of your female applicants, there is disparate treatment of a protected segment of the population.

Emphasizing Diversity and Working with a Multicultural Workforce

The increased diversity of today's workforce has brought many benefits to business in the form of varying viewpoints and a wider range of skills and talents. It has also brought many challenges as companies strive to accommodate these viewpoints and incorporate them into the fabric of their workplace. The labor force is now represented more by women and minorities than by the "average white male." In contrast to the perceived notion that companies are finding ways to continue discriminatory practices, many companies today are actively trying to build a diverse workforce by new recruitment practices. They recognize that diversity, rather than an additional human resource cost is an asset. Once both the company and its employees have accepted the reality of a diverse workforce, the organization will be able to take advantage of its benefits. Single parents, older workers, minorities, women, and the disabled offer a vast pool of talent. Many single parents are forced to work menial jobs or to work only part-time because of childcare issues. Companies can be proactive in attracting this workforce by initiating flexible time schedules, job-sharing, and even on-site childcare.

Most companies today recognize that the needs of the diverse workforce alter the requirements for benefits. A single parent with a child may feel cheated if the company pays for full family coverage for one worker, while hers only pays for parent and child coverage. An older worker may not require coverage at all if he is covered by a retirement plan. These situations have led to the development of cafeteria-style benefit plans in which employees receive a set amount and can choose among various options based on their needs. Older workers are becoming more attractive candidates as the job market gets tighter. Employers who have hired them find that intellectual skills and creativity are not diminished. Older employees have better attendance, are more loyal, and are more satisfied with their jobs than their younger counterparts.

Companies are formulating plans to attract more minorities and women by changing policies, offering flexible work plans, and offering remedial programs in basic education. Many companies, instead of finding ways of proving undue hardship to accommodate the handicapped, are renovating facilities to accommodate the wheelchair bound, the visually and hearing-impaired, and the mentally challenged.

Companies also have to find ways to accommodate a workforce with different cultural and language backgrounds. Offering language courses and providing translated training manuals can allow workers from various backgrounds to function in the organization. To promote acceptance in the organization, diversity must be managed from a humane perspective.

It is a challenge to incorporate the benefits of a culturally diverse workforce while avoiding the problems of prejudice. The concept of diversity has to become a cultural adaptation rather than a regulation. One of the first steps required to ensure that diversity becomes an integral part of an organization is to put strong guidance in place. If the members of an organization see that the effort is serious enough to be headed by a senior member of management, the message is more readily accepted. In a smaller company, the owner will have to spearhead the effort. The company will need to do a thorough assessment of its current diversity status, including what kind of programs are already in place to encourage diversity which can be increased through adaptive recruitment campaigns (especially for senior management and board members) as well as through training for current employees. One major bank has a diversity month, in which members of the various cultural communities are invited to exhibit their art, culture, and food on different days. Local community groups provide a glimpse of these cultures as a children's dance troupe performs traditional Indian dances or a musician entertains the lunch crowd with Spanish guitar. To ensure that diversity is a managed aspect of the corporation, it should be targeted as a goal by supervisors. Once a diversity program has been initiated, put a system in place to monitor attitudes and to determine how the program is succeeding.

One of the first places the diversity message should appear is in the employee handbook. Most companies state that they are "equal opportunity employers," (any applicant regardless of race, color, sex, religion, national origin, or age has an equal chance for employment and advancement in the company), but some may take the concept further, declaring diversity as one of their missions and developing a mission statement that recognizes the essential benefit and justice in a multicultural workforce. Some employers choose to manage diversity through affirmative action which means it actively hires and promotes workers in protected groups such as women and minorities. Affirmative action does have some risks and has been struck down in some court cases. To be safe, a company is protected by using a good faith system in which the firm works to eliminate barriers to hiring and to promoting protected groups, without setting actual rates on the numbers hired.

With today's global economy and expanded consumer base, a diverse workforce can play a major role in a company's competitiveness. Companies and human resource professionals should recognize that diversity is not only a desirable goal, but also a profitable one.

Training to Prevent Discrimination

Discrimination often exhibits itself in its ugliest forms: harassment and ill treatment. Despite a company's best efforts to foster a diverse workplace and to attempt to create a more diverse employee base through affirmation action, it is the individual employee — a supervisor, manager, or co-worker — who is ultimately responsible for employee relations. Ironically, fostering diversity and affirmative action may cause some employees to be jealous and resentful, prompting vindictiveness.

The first step in preventing discrimination and harassment is to have a strongly worded official policy that forbids it. An anti-harassment and discrimination policy should prohibit any kind of harassment based on race, national origin, religion, sex, age, disability, veteran status, or marital status. In addition to the costs to the company in terms of poor morale and lost productivity, discrimination and harassment can cost a company millions of dollars in legal damages if it is accused of engaging in discriminatory or harassing practices. A company's anti-discrimination policy should be clear that it does not tolerate this behavior, and any reports will be investigated, and violations will be handled severely. It should also have clear instructions that complaints should be reported to the human resource department, not to supervisors or department heads. Having a strong policy will help protect a company against discrimination and harassment lawsuits, but it is still no guarantee. Creating a work environment that fosters diversity and understanding through training and example will be a stronger deterrent to harassment than written policies. Actions speak louder than words.

Sexual harassment is one of the most complex aspects of illegal harassment because it takes many forms, some of them very subtle. Most sexual harassment charges are filed by women, but the victims can be men, and the harasser does not necessarily have to be of the opposite sex. In addition, the person suffering the perceived harassment does not have to be the one who bore the brunt of the incident, but another who was affected by it. An accused harasser does not necessarily have to be in a supervisory role for the company to be considered complicit in the harassment. If co-workers are harassing each other, they are construed to be representing the company if the company is doing nothing to prevent it. There are two types of sexual harassment: quid pro quo and hostile environment. Quid pro quo is the more blatant of the two, the kind in which a supervisor will request sexual favors in return for a raise or a promotion. Hostile environment covers most sexual harassment today, describing an environment of sexual comments, dirty jokes, (verbal or e-mail), and physical contact that is sexual in nature. The definition of a hostile environment that is considered sexually harassing is that it is "unwelcome, severe, and pervasive in the workplace" (*The HR Answer Book*, Shawn Smith, J.D. and Rebecca Mazin). If anyone voices an objection, the behavior must be addressed. For example, an atmosphere where street language, which may be offensive to some, is consistently used can be considered a hostile environment if someone objects to it, even if this situation has been tolerated in the past. The employer has an obligation to protect employees against a hostile environment, even when it is not created by an employee of the company. The salesman or delivery person who is delivering naughty jokes should not be allowed to continue this behavior if anyone finds it offensive. Many times harassers have tried to prove that a consensual sexual relationship existed, but if the events leading to the relationship included being threatened with the loss of a job, the victim may have a legitimate claim. Even if the relationship was initially consensual, once it is not, it is sexual harassment. An employer is responsible for sexual harassment if the harassment can be proven to result in any change in employment status, including firing, demotion, unwanted transfer, or a lack of a promotion.

Sexual harassment receives the most attention, but harassment because of race, religion, or national origin should not be tolerated and is prohibited by Title VII. Ethnic slurs, jokes targeting certain ethnic or national groups, or the use of derogatory terms to refer to certain groups should not be allowed in the workplace. Besides illegal, this type of behavior is demeaning to those groups and will affect both employee morale and productivity.

Policies on Dating and Marriage

Because people spend most of their waking hours at work, office romances blossom. As long as the contact between the employees is consensual and does not interfere with work, most companies do not interfere. Problems do arise, however, if the parties are in the same department, especially if there is an employee-supervisor relationship. Obviously, this may lead to charges of favoritism. For this reason, many companies prohibit married couples, or even relatives, from working in the same department or in positions in which they have to work together, even if in different departments. A further complication arises if two employees who work together and who are dating get married. Who gets transferred or has to leave the company? If a company requires the least senior of the two to make the change, this can become a sensitive discrimination issue. Some states now have laws that prohibit discrimination based on marital status. Many companies choose to let the couple decide who will leave or be transferred.

COMPANY: Auxiliary Services Corporation

Michelle K. Brackin, Human Resources Manager

Our employees enjoy health, dental, and vision insurance, discounted meals, and paid time off. All new employees also train with a supervisor, and we hold an orientation each semester that covers a great deal information, including food sanitation and occupational safety training. All employees have a three-month initial performance evaluation, and non union employees annually receive a performance evaluation based on 20 criteria.

Additionally, we annually recognize one employee who provides exceptional customer service and one department. The employee receives a plaque, write up in the newsletter, and a token gift.

We keep our employees abreast of all the latest information and news through an annual employee meeting, an employee newsletter, orientation for new employees, and posters. To receive feedback and suggestions from our employees, we have a column in our employee newsletter that requests employees to submit questions for management to answer. We also have a notice of an open-door policy in our employee handbook.

Michelle K. Brackin, Human Resources Manager
Auxiliary Services Corporation
Neubig Hall SUNY Cortland • Cortland, NY 13045
Brackinm@cortland.edu • Ascweb.cortland.edu
Phone: 607-753-2431

CHAPTER 11

Establishing Compensation Plans

The term "compensation" refers to any form of pay or reward given in exchange for employment services. Compensation refers to salaries, wages, bonuses, commission, and financial benefits. Certain aspects of compensation are covered by law. The Fair Labor Standards Act (FSLA) legislates minimum wage, overtime, and maximum hours. The Equal Pay Act legislates compensation discrimination based on sex, and the Employee Retirement Income Security Act (ERISA) provides for the protection of employee pension plans in the public sector. If an employer does not offer a pension plan, it will not be covered under ERISA. Outside of minimum wage and discrimination laws and the treatment of pension plans, employers are fairly free to set whatever compensation they think is just.

Most companies strive to set compensation policies both that are competitive in the marketplace to attract the best candidates and that are aligned along levels of responsibility. The scarcity or surplus of employees in certain fields will push wages up or down, and geography influences salary levels dramatically. The cost-of-living differences in different parts of the country may make setting equitable wage levels difficult for companies with locations across the country and across the world.

A tool that many companies use to establish pay rates is the salary survey. Many professional organizations, like chambers of commerce and industry organizations, conduct surveys wherein they request members to submit ranges of salaries for different types of employment. Another way for an employer to gauge what kind of salary to offer when a position opens is to check the want ads in the geographic area of the job. This chore has become easier with the advent of Internet recruiting, since positions in different areas of the country can be viewed easily. This system may work in a small company when only one position at a time needs to be filled, but in an environment where the accounting department has 20 employees, each with varying levels of skills and experience, it becomes more difficult to set levels of salary.

A number of factors will affect these levels. First of all, employees who have been with the company may not have the same level of education as a new hire, yet will be paid more because of annual increases. Conversely, new hires may join the company at a higher level of pay because the company needs to stay competitive in the hiring market. This is increasingly common in fields in which there is a labor shortage. Many companies may initiate "parity" increases for existing employees when new employees receive higher salaries because of market considerations. The company that does not do this risks losing valued employees who will now enter this market at higher rates.

Establishing Salary Ranges

Most companies try to establish pay tiers, or grades, to make the structure fairer and more manageable. An analysis of the skills and efforts required, responsibilities assumed, and working conditions in each job will match like to like, allowing a company to fix different pay grades based on these factors. Pay grades may be based on the current salaries that are paid in these positions, or on an analysis based on pay surveys in the field, or a combination of both. Establishing pay grades will make it easier for managers to negotiate with potential new hires. It would be a nightmare in a large company if each position's salary had to be calculated and negotiated individually. In most cases, the pay grades have salary ranges attached to them so that managers have some flexibility in the negotiation process.

Most of these solutions apply to rank-and-file workers.

Executive, managerial, and professional positions may be managed somewhat differently, but the concept is the same: to attract and keep the best employees. However, setting pay scales may be more difficult since managerial duties are harder to quantify, so managers are usually rewarded for their ability rather than for the amount of work produced. The theory is that executive compensation is more directly related to the organization's results than to other employees' salaries. However, there have been some recent grumblings among stockholders when executive compensation is in the stratosphere while the company profits are plummeting. Recent events in such high-profile corporate failures as Enron and Worldcom have forced many boards to re-examine their executive compensation policies. Professional positions also pose unique problems because they emphasize creativity and their contribution is only seen as part of the total effort of the company. A new drug will be successful only if both the advertising and sales departments do their jobs.

Many companies today recognize that nonwage benefits represent a valuable attraction to most employees. Such benefits as vacation, sick, and personal days; health, dental, prescription, vision, and life insurance; and contributions to pension, stock options, and 401(k) plans can add considerably to a total compensation package. At the upper level of management, additional perks may be added to the compensation plan such as company cars or planes, country club memberships, and additional residences. Benefits will be further discussed in Chapter 13.

Performance Incentives

In many fields, most notably in sales, bonuses and incentives are an integral part of the salary package. Many companies establish bonuses as a flat dollar amount that is awarded once a year, usually at the holidays. Since holiday bonuses are based on the company's results for the year, they are not guaranteed and therefore do not serve as a recruitment tool. Sales bonuses, however, are usually negotiated as part of a total compensation package and are guaranteed as long as established sales targets are met.

Some companies also offer short-term bonuses for special projects or initiatives. A company may have a bonus that employees share if there are three consecutive months without an accident, for example. Other short-term bonus plans may reward improved customer satisfaction. These kinds of incentive plans are designed to encourage employees to give that "something extra" and may be limited in scope and duration. Other bonuses that companies grant are sign-on bonuses, especially in tight labor markets, and retention bonuses when a company is being restructured or entering into a merger.

Payroll

State law regulates when, where, how, and how often employees must be paid. Most of the time, employees must be paid by cash or negotiable check (direct deposit is, of course, tantamount to a negotiable check). Unless otherwise agreed upon, pay must be made at a reasonable place for the employee to obtain it, and most states require that employees be paid at a minimum of twice monthly. Some states have only monthly requirements.

Pay and payroll are the most sensitive issues in the corporate environment. Few employees believe they are adequately compensated, and they often think that everyone else makes more than they do. All of the best efforts at equitable compensation scales and systems will not eliminate this quirk of human nature. Salary is often perceived as the measure of a person's worth, and many employees as well as companies treat the issue with secrecy, which often leads to misinformation. Given the sensitive nature of their pay, it is understandable that most employees are sensitive about their paycheck and the entire issue of payroll. It is incumbent upon a company, and the human resource department of the company, to handle payroll issues with the utmost sensitivity, care, and discretion. Many companies, even relatively small ones, subscribe to automated payroll systems that have now become inexpensive because of the mass volume of transactions. This usually results in fewer problems in terms of calculations, and the payroll department employees do not have to be payroll tax experts to process a payroll. Often, a payroll processing module may be part of an overall human resource information system that tracks and monitors many issues regarding human resources, including personal information, salary information and job status, performance review outcomes and schedules for performance reviews, benefit information, emergency contact information, records of skills and training, and so on.

The Fair Labor Standards Act (FLSA) requires employers to keep payroll records for three years. Payroll records, which include time cards or sheets; W-4 and 941 forms; records for overtime, commissions, or bonuses; garnishments; and the employer copy of annual W-2 forms, should be kept separate from the other personnel files.

After an employee is hired, all of the information for his or her pay should be entered into the payroll records, including name, Social Security number, address, salary basis (hourly or salaried, exempt from overtime or nonexempt), rate of pay, and relevant deductions and tax exemptions. This information is critical, and usually will be entered by a payroll clerk. It is imperative that the information is entered correctly and double-checked. Almost nothing will sour the new relationship between the employee and the employer more quickly than being paid at the wrong rate or having an incorrect deduction for benefits or taxes. Even though any such error can be corrected, some errors may not even be noticed until much later. If a Social Security number is incorrectly input, the employee may not notice it until a W-2 wage statement is issued. The same may occur with the employee's address, since so many employees pick up their paychecks or have them directly deposited to their banks.

Once payroll records have been properly entered,

continuous and scrupulous care must be given to the weekly or bi-weekly payroll entries. Managers must have clear instructions on how to process and submit time cards for hourly employees, carefully calculating hours that may be eligible for overtime. The payroll department will know how to calculate overtime, or it may be automatically calculated by a payroll system (at the rate of 1.5 times the nonexempt employee's base rate for any hours worked over 40 in a week), but it will be up to the manager to submit accurate hours worked in order for these calculations to be made. Once again, it becomes an extremely sensitive issue if an employee thinks he was cheated out of his overtime, when it was really just an error on the part of the supervisor or the payroll clerk. Regardless of the logic, or lack of it, many employees are convinced they are personally targeted when errors occur. In addition, the penalties for failure to pay correct overtime wages can be severe. The payroll or human resource department will also be responsible for paying and monitoring such benefit days as holidays, personal, sick, and vacation days.

Most payroll deductions are either mandated by the government (federal and state income taxes, unemployment, and Social Security taxes) or are agreed upon by the employee (deductions for health, dental, prescription, vision, and life insurance as well as contributions to pension, stock options, or 401(k) plans). The employer must maintain proper documentation showing that the employee has authorized any deductions to his salary, outside of mandatory ones. Attachments against wages (garnishments) can be made if the employer receives a bona fide court order demanding payment of a judgment. These judgments usually represent student loans, consumer credit debt, or support payments. The Consumer Credit Protection act places a limit on the amount that can be deducted from an employee's paycheck to pay a judgment. The employer is required to make the deduction according to a formula that is supplied by the ordering agency.

Miscellaneous: Sales Commissions, Piece Work, Stock Options

Not all employees are paid an hourly rate for the length of time they are at their place of work. Many salespeople are compensated by a base rate of pay and commissions on their sales. The commission is usually a percentage of the sales price of the product or service the salesperson is credited with selling. There are various arrangements regarding sales commissions; some salespeople receive only their commissions and no base pay, while others receive a combination. Many commissioned salespeople work on a "draw." In other words, they take a fixed amount each pay period that is "drawn" against their total commissions. This draw is adjusted from time to time to reflect actual commissions earned.

Just as salespeople are not paid by the hour, many employees in certain industries are paid by the amount of product they produce. This is known as piece work.

The original idea behind piece work was to motivate employees to produce more, so wages were based solely on the amount produced by the worker. This type of pay structure is not used as extensively as it used to be, but it is still common in certain industries, including the garment industry. Even in cases where employees are paid by the piece, wage and hour laws require that total pay divided by the number of hours worked in a period must average out to at least the minimum hourly rate set by law.

The concept of rewarding employees in a way that is directly related to the success of the company was the original concept of piecework, but the modern way of rewarding employees more likely takes the form of stock options. Stock options give employees the right to purchase shares in the company at a fixed price. Employees do not have the obligation to buy the shares, but if the price of the stock goes up, they can buy the shares at the original price (exercise their option) and sell them at the higher price. However, if the price never goes above the option price, there may be no value. Stock options may have originally been designed for executive compensation packages, but more and more companies are offering them to all of their employees. They are especially popular in high-tech and computer companies. Start-up companies may offer stock options to employees in lieu of a bonus, but until the company goes public, the option has no value since the shares cannot be sold on a public stock exchange. However, this method has made many millionaires out of ordinary employees who were able to hold on to their options until the firm went public and then sell them at a lucrative price. This phenomenon was common in dotcom and computer start-up companies. These programs must comply with tax laws and are subject to Securities and Exchange Commission regulations, so it is advisable to consult legal and tax experts if a company is considering such a plan.

Mike Smith, SPHR
www.mikesmith-hr.com

To evaluate employees, we have an objec-
tives-based performance review system in
which we rank employees with similar job
scopes within vice presidential groups. We
annually conduct employee performance appraisals. To recognize
exemplary employees, we offer Spot Awards, Presidential Awards
(a few a year worth $10,000 each), Annual Awards for dozens of
categories, and individual and team awards ranging from $3,000 to
$25,000.

To maintain employee safety at all times, Safety Group keeps us
alert to potential problems. Fortunately, staying safe is not that
hard for an almost all white-collar operation.

One problem we've consistently faced is employees focusing too
narrowly on their job without considering implications of their
actions on other parts of the organization or the customers.

> *Mike Smith, SPHR*
> *Six Sigma Certified Black Belt*
> *www.mikesmith-hr.com*

CHAPTER 12

Employee Retention

One of the most difficult tasks facing any company is retaining good employees. To do so, a company must recognize performance, promote morale, and build corporate loyalty. After attaining the basic needs of fair compensation and benefits, a safe work environment, and adequate training to do a good job, most employees find that being recognized for their contributions is one of the most important aspects of their job. However, if the basics of fair treatment and equitable compensation are not a part of the corporate philosophy, no recognition program will compensate for a deficiency in good corporate governance.

Employee Recognition Programs

How, then, does a company make sure that employees are

recognized for their contributions? Most companies would like to initiate an employee recognition program but do not know where to start. One of the main points that should be established is that a cookie-cutter approach will not work, because different types of employees want to be recognized in different ways. The kinds of performance that the company wants to recognize and reward need to be examined, and the type of rewards that will work best with each group of employees needs to be determined. One of the best ways to find out what will work for your employees is to ask for their input. The common wisdom is that most employees would like to be rewarded in such tangible ways as financial rewards or prizes. However, many times, employees are most rewarded with simple praise or with other recognition that does not require a financial outlay by the company. The program need not even be a formal one.

Frequently showing support and appreciation for a job well-done will work wonders. Training managers to recognize and acknowledge good performance by their staff may be one of the most valuable tools a company can use to keep good employees. In addition, giving employees more latitude in the decision-making process, giving teams of employees more autonomy, and bringing employees into the communication processes of the company have been shown to increase involvement and a sense of connection with the company. An employee is more likely to stay with a company if he or she feels truly a part of it. Many believe this is one of the reasons people stayed with companies for most of their lives years ago;

many of those companies were small businesses, and the owners knew each of their employees and treated them as family. This "being part of a family" approach is at the heart of many current initiatives to make the employee feel as though he or she belongs.

If a company wants to initiate a recognition program, it must first look at what kind of performance the company wants to reward. It is important that the reward program is in sync with the goals of the corporation. It is, therefore, important to have the human resource department design and administer the program. Individual departments may have their own ideas about what kind of behavior or performance should be rewarded. They may, however, not be in the best interest of the whole company, as some managers may try to protect their little pond at the cost of company goals. The type and costs of these programs must be coordinated and made fair so that one department will not be singled out to the exclusion of other departments. All must feel that they are contributing to the success of the company, even if their contribution is not as direct as that of others. For these reasons, a central, administrative department, such as the human resource department, is best suited to oversee these programs.

Any program should be thoroughly examined to make sure that it rewards superior performance, not just average performance; otherwise it will lose its impact and value. However, if it is an impossible goal that no one can reach, it will have no benefit or value.

Another criterion that should be met when administering recognition programs is that they must be well-communicated. The way the award is determined must be clear and well-defined. When it is not clear to all concerned how the award will be determined (or who will determine it), dissention and discord will follow. Large companies may find the administration of rewards programs cumbersome, which is a great risk to a company since it may mean some people are excluded if the program is not carefully administered. A solution may be to have an outside company administer the policy. This is frequently the solution for anniversary-recognition or level-of-sales programs, in which the recipient is automatically eligible for a gift on an anniversary date or at a certain dollar value of sales.

Many companies reward good attendance, especially if they have generous sick-day benefits programs. Employees are encouraged not to use their sick days if they are "bought back" by the company. This rewards the employee for not using a sick day, and the company is not losing an employee for a day. This works especially well in "use it or lose it" types of sick day policies. Many employees will use all their sick days whether they need to or not if there is no incentive not to use them.

Length-of-service awards are rightly given a place of distinction within a company. Frequently vacation time is accrued based on an employee's length of service and is a strong incentive for a worker to stay with a company. Despite other advantages, an employee will seriously weigh the decision to change jobs if it means going from five weeks of vacation with his or her long-time company to two weeks with a new employer. Also, there is no better way for a company to send a message that staying with the company is important than to recognize a milestone such as a tenth or twenty-fifth anniversary of an employee. There is no better way to make employees feel an important part of an organization than by having the senior management of the company applaud their years of service!

If a company is trying to lower its insurance and worker's compensation claims, it may initiate a "safety first" program. In the most common programs, a department or plant shares a monetary reward for being accident free. Frequently a factory floor will have a sign proclaiming "90 days without an accident!" This same type of group cash incentive can work extremely well if a firm is trying to get a project out on a tight schedule. A reward can be offered if the deadline is met, but a greater reward is promised if the project is completed ahead of schedule. Many times a company will try to launch a new product or service and will give a specific reward to the employee who can sell the most of the new product or service. An additional type of reward may be tied to an add-on of a product or service. If a certain product is a best seller, the company may try to piggyback on the popularity of the product or service by selling something related to it. Service agreements on entertainment equipment or appliances are frequently used in this way. A salesperson may receive an additional bonus for the sale of the service agreement, over and above the commission for the sale of the product. This type of reward program risks emphasizing short-term results over long-term success, and it needs to be carefully balanced with other programs in the company. Again, be sure the type of reward is in agreement with the way the company wants to run its business. If a team approach is paramount, recognition awards should concentrate on accomplishments that require shared responsibility.

Another successful incentive that serves recruitment purposes while rewarding current employees at the same time is an employment referral program. Current employees are rewarded for bringing in new employees. Using the employee bulletin, newsletter, or intranet site, notify employees of any openings and of the qualifications for them. Promptly follow up with employees as to the status of anyone they have recommended. If a new hire does work out, distribute rewards promptly and make sure that recognition is given to the referring employee. This will not only make him or her feel like a contributing part of the organization, but it also will encourage others to participate.

There are a number of standard recognition programs that have been used successfully by many companies for years. Companies have given gifts ranging from such tokens as mugs, pens, plaques, or gift certificates to more formal recognition such as honorary dinners or large cash or merchandise rewards. The most important thing is that the value of the award, as it is recognized by the recipient, corresponds to the value of his or her performance. A company that values longevity will justify sending a long-standing employee on an all-expenses paid trip; while another company may consider a plaque or a watch an ample reward for length of service but would send its top salesperson on an expensive trip.

Work-Life Balance

In the 20th and 21st centuries, changes in family makeup and lifestyle have revolutionized the workplace. There are more families in which both parents work, more full-time working women, and more single-parent homes. These changes in the workforce have challenged corporations to find ways to accommodate the demands of home life while allowing employees to be contributing members of the corporate team. Some companies have accommodated this need grudgingly, recognizing that it is the only way they will attract and retain good employees; others have enthusiastically embraced work-life balance programs and have actively sought recognition as a family-friendly employer. Many solutions have been generated to create a family-friendly environment. In *Low-Cost Strategies for Employee Retention* Maureen Hannay and Melissa Northam cite a number of them:

- On-site childcare.

- Fitness and medical facilities.

- Flexible work schedules.

- Telecommuting (including loan programs for home computers).

- Sabbaticals.

- Concierge services.

Large employers or companies with a large female workforce may find it in their own as well as their employees' best interest to have on-site childcare. The employee pays for the childcare, but it may be less expensive because it is subsidized by the company. It is also comforting for a parent to know the child is nearby in case of a problem. Commuting is easier as well, since the parent does not have to go to a different location before going to work.

In the interest of the health of their employees, many large organizations offer fitness facilities. Not surprisingly, many organizations in the health field, including pharmaceutical firms, hospitals, and health insurance companies, are at the forefront of this concept. Employees come in early to work out, exercise over lunch break, or stay late to get in a workout. Many of these arrangements are also subsidized and therefore less expensive for the employee. Some of these employers also offer health clinics on-site. This reduces time off for employees because they do not have to take an entire day off for a doctor's appointment, and it helps health maintenance because employees are more likely to go to the clinic because it is easier and frequently less expensive.

Alternate work arrangements, including flexible work schedules, allow an employee to work outside the core hours of the company, as long as the same number of hours is maintained. In the typical nine-to-five environment, a parent of school-aged children may prefer to come in early and leave in time to meet the children when they arrive home from school. Flexible schedule arrangements can be ongoing or on an as-needed basis. For instance, an employee with a sick or elderly parent may need to arrive late because of the schedule of a home health aide. If that need changes, the employee's hours may return to normal. Another variation in alternate work arrangements is the compressed work week, in which an employee works the same number of hours in a week but in fewer days. Many employees appreciate the value of having an extra day off and are willing to extend the length of the other four working days. Some other companies may offer job sharing in which two individuals work part-time doing the same job. Benefits are prorated, based on hours worked. In this type of arrangement, an hour or so a day may overlap to ensure coordination of duties.

Telecommuting is working off-site. It is one of the most difficult programs to implement because so many employers feel they are unable to monitor the productivity of an employee who is not on-site. These programs are more suited to jobs in which results are easily measurable, such as sales, when a great deal of time is already spent away from the office. Telecommuting is suited to individuals who can work independently with little direction. A company must examine expenses, safety, and security of information before telecommuting can be considered a viable alternative to the standard workweek.

Well-established in the academic world, sabbaticals are intended to allow an employee to pursue his field of study to refresh his professional knowledge. The sabbatical has been transferred to the corporate world to allow for extended time off simply to "recharge" or to pursue reading and study that will advance the employee's business knowledge, further contributing to the company's success.

Concierge services are a relatively new innovation, first introduced in the creative fields. Now used as a way to recruit highly sought-after candidates, especially in the sales and computer technology fields, concierge services are offered to lighten the burden of everyday chores. These services will pick up dry cleaning, make appointments and reservations, walk pets, and even send a shoe polisher or masseur to the office for the employee. The concept is based on the theory that when creative people are freed from the mundane, they will be more creative.

Some leave programs have been legislated by national or state law, including maternity leave and family medical leave. Motivated employers have sometimes expanded these programs to be longer in duration or to include paid benefits. As an employee-retention tool, work-life benefits have been cited by employees as one of the most important benefits. Although there is no indisputable proof that such programs improve job performance or productivity, anecdotal evidence suggests that employees are less stressed and more satisfied at work, and therefore more loyal and motivated.

COMPANY: New Horizons Community Credit Union

Linda Konstan, Vice President of Human Resources

Employees receive performance reviews after the first six months, and then annually based on various metrics. We also have recognition programs for outstanding employees. For example, we have an incentive plan for some frontline employees (based on sales and referrals). We also have various fun incentives based on extraordinary work: gift cards, flowers, photo frames that say "superstar," handing out Kudos candy bars, bringing trays of food to departments, 30-second parades, jeans days, and special dress days.

Of course, as with any company, we do have to confront performance issues. For example, gossip and rumors are always a tricky issue to deal with. We put a stop to that immediately and hope that our open-door policy will make employees realize that they can go to management with any problem.

Linda Konstan is also President of an HR consulting firm for small businesses: LMK Associates, 303-722-8525, Lkonstan@juno.com

Linda Konstan, Vice President of Human Resources
New Horizons Community Credit Union
99 South Broadway • Denver, CO 80209
303-744-3535 • www.newhorizonsccu.org

CHAPTER 13

Employee Benefits

One of the most complex areas of human resource management today is employee benefits. An employee benefit is any form of compensation outside of the employee's pay. Gone are the days when a company offered only a hospital plan and a pension to their employees. The job market has become increasingly competitive, so additional benefits are offered as enticements. In addition, there is no longer an "average" employee for whom the identical benefit package will work across the board. Finally, the government dictates many of the aspects of employee benefits. Today an employee who is covered under his spouse's health care plan may opt not to take advantage of his own company's plan. However, he may still feel entitled to a comparable benefit and would object if he were not offered something in return for opting out of the health plan. Various state and local governments either mandate certain benefits or oversee the administration of certain benefits.

Mandated Benefits:
Social Security, Unemployment,
Workers' Compensation, Medical Leaves

The Social Security Administration was created in 1935 when President Franklin D. Roosevelt signed the Social Security Act into law. Partially as a reaction to the Great Depression, the federal government realized it was important that all workers be provided with a basic retirement benefit. Social Security now also includes Medicare to provide health care benefits for retired individuals. If a worker was born in 1929 or later, he needs to have worked for at least 10 years to be eligible for retirement benefits. If he was born before 1938, his "full retirement age" is 65. But, because of longer life expectancies, the full retirement age is increasing for people born after 1938, scheduled to rise gradually to 67. A worker may start collecting his Social Security benefits as early as age 62, but the amount received each month will be less than if he started collecting at full retirement age. Social Security retirement and Medicare benefits are funded by payroll taxes paid by both the employer and the employee. The employer is required by law to deduct 7.65 percent of an employee's salary and to match 7.65 percent, to a total contribution of 15.3 percent. The deduction changes after a certain income ceiling. The employee will receive an annual statement showing how much he has paid into Social Security and what he can expect his benefit to be at any given retirement age, increasing the longer retirement is delayed.

Since mandatory retirement is against the law, an employer may have employees who are eligible to collect Social Security and who still earn a salary. (Social Security benefits also are affected by salary earned.) An employee has a choice of either supplementing his salary with a Social Security check or delaying his declared retirement in order to increase his monthly benefit when he does retire. Many older workers are continuing to work, either to increase their benefit, out of boredom, or because their Social Security earnings are not enough to live on. Employers, especially in tight job markets, are also learning the benefits of retaining or hiring an older workforce, who may have years of knowledge and experience combined with sterling work ethics, which are increasingly rare. For more information on Social Security benefits, visit www.ssa.gov.

The Social Security Act of 1935 also created unemployment insurance. Each state runs its own unemployment program under the federal guidelines. Most states require the employer to fund the entire cost of unemployment insurance, with the rates based on the company's "experience rating." This rating is based on the employment history of the company. The more the company has fired or laid off employees, the higher its rate will be. This factor forces many companies to be cautious about hiring additional help in case there is a downturn and they need to lay off workers. The rating also accounts for one of the reasons many companies hold onto employees who should be let go because of poor performance. Each state's unemployment insurance program is different, but, for the most part, if an employee has worked for an employer for a certain minimum length of time and is let go, he or she can collect unemployment insurance while seeking a new job. The length of time he or she can collect differs, and in times of serious national unemployment levels, the length of time is extended. Unemployment insurance agencies also assist the unemployed in finding new jobs.

Workers' compensation is an insurance program operated by the state that provides protection to employees who have been injured on the job. Again, since it is state run, there are differences state to state, but in general, workers' compensation pays the medical bills related to the injury, provides replacement income, and will pay a lump sum benefit to the family if the worker dies as a result of his or her injuries. The program works in a manner similar to unemployment insurance whereby both the employer and the employee pay into the fund. The employer's contribution is based on its experience rating; that is, how many claims it has had against it. It is good business sense to maintain an employee safety program, both to keep your employees safe and to keep your workers' compensation contributions and insurance premiums (if the company has a private workers' compensation insurance program) low. Many states now recognize illnesses, not just injuries, as work-related. The typical workers' compensation case years ago may have been someone falling off a ladder or injuring his hand in a machine. Today, it could as easily be heart disease from work-induced stress, carpal tunnel from repetitive computer chores, or depression from a mentally unhealthy work environment. Most employers and insurance companies recognize that fraudulent workers' comp insurance claims are rising, adding to the cost of the insurance and are vigilant about exposing them.

Most companies have leave-of-absence policies that allow employees to take time off (usually for medical reasons) without losing their employment status. Depending on the company's policy, this leave may or may not provide pay during this period. The Family Medical Leave Act (FMLA), or Public Law 103-3, enacted in 1993, legislates that companies with 50 or more employees grant employees up to 12 weeks' unpaid leave to care for newly born or adopted children; to care for a child, parent, or spouse with a serious health condition; or for the employee's own serious health condition that prevents him or her from working. Under this law, the employer must maintain the employee's health insurance coverage, and the employee retains the right to the same or similar job when he or she returns to work. A company's own leave policy may work in conjunction with FMLA, but it can never cover less than the law requires. Some states have also passed medical leave acts that may be more generous than the federal one; a company must comply with the law of its state, even if it provides a greater benefit than the federal one. In some cases, a combination of the two may be necessary. For instance, the New Jersey Family Leave Act can be induced to care for a newborn after the employee has been on leave under FMLA for her own serious health condition that prevented her from working (pregnancy).

Voluntary Benefits: Sick Days, Vacations, Personal Days, Holidays, Leaves

There are many reasons for a company to offer paid or unpaid time off to its employees beyond the requirements of the law. If employees are forced to work day after day, without respite, the health of both the employees and the company suffers. In addition, many companies use generous sick or vacation policies as a recruitment tool. Most companies now consider such a benefit as part of a standard package — and it is just a question of how much time is granted and administered. It is important to have a clearly defined policy to control abuses and to apply the policy evenly to prevent accusations of discrimination. Most companies allow a certain number of paid sick days per year, with a limit on how many consecutive days may be taken before the period becomes a "leave" period, which is covered by a different policy. As we have seen in Chapter 12, some companies also treat the unused portion of the sick leave policy as an incentive to come to work in a "buy back" policy.

Unlike a sick-day policy that should be applied evenly to all employees, vacation policies are usually related to an employee's length of service. This can be a valuable retention tool, as mentioned earlier. Usually, vacation increments are increased weekly on important seniority milestones. A company that starts employees with two weeks of vacation the first year may give three weeks starting the fifth year, four weeks starting the tenth year, and so on. Some companies allow employees to carry vacation over from one year to another. Wise policies have a limit on how much vacation time can be carried forward.

Personal days allow an employee to use a paid benefit day to attend to personal business. Many times, these personal days can be used incrementally; that is, a few hours to have a car repaired or an afternoon to attend a child's school play. Many times, sick days, vacation days, and personal days are bundled together and called "benefit days," and the employee has no obligation to report how the private time is used. However, most companies like to specify that vacation days require advance notice so that they don't disrupt business.

If a company has a leave policy that is more generous than the applicable state or federal policy applicable, it may apply its policy to situations that fall outside of FMLA policy. In addition to illness or military leaves covered under the law, a company's leave policy may cover education or travel and may provide income for part of the period. If the company decides to administer this type of policy on a case-by-case basis, it should be careful to avoid any appearance of discrimination.

Involuntary Benefits: Health, Dental, Life, and Disability Insurance and Cafeteria Plans

Most types of employee insurance, especially health insurance, have become big business for insurance companies, a big attraction for employees, and a big headache for employers. Nevertheless, if a company wants to attract and keep top talent, it must be competitive and offer not only such standard benefits as health and dental insurance, but also life insurance and disability insurance. These programs may be paid for by the employer or funded by a mixture of employee co-insurance and employer funding. In addition, many employers offer "cafeteria plans" in which the employee chooses the right options for himself and his family.

Health insurance is the most sought-after and the most expensive employment benefit. Companies are constantly faced with the challenge of offering competitive health benefits to employees while keeping the costs down. The resulting plans are staggering in their variety because increasing a benefit in one way that may benefit the majority of a company's staff may result in a higher cost for something else. Companies have the option of offering traditional health insurance plans or managed care plans (HMOs), a choice between them, or a combination of both. In a traditional health insurance plan, an employee goes to any doctor he chooses, and he pays the bill until he has reached his "deductible." After that, there is a cost-sharing plan (co-pay) where the insurance pays the larger part of the bills and the employee the smaller: traditionally 80 percent and 20 percent.

The cost of the premium adjusts upward or downward based on the size of the deductible and the percentage the insurance company pays. A small company with a young workforce may opt to keep premiums low by having a large deductible, with the philosophy that they will not use the benefit much. Managed care plans require that the employee go to a doctor or health care facility "in the network" and pay a much lower, fixed amount per visit, regardless of the doctor bill. This type of health insurance is tightly controlled to reduce costs to the insurance company, and the medical providers in the network agree to reduced payments in exchange for a guaranteed roster of patients. There is also a hybrid of the two that treats the employee as in the managed care network, with a fixed per-visit cost, but allows him to go outside the network when desired, in which case the insurance becomes a traditional plan with a co-insurance and co-pay. An employee who does not have a preference for his general care practitioner but insists on a certain dermatologist, for example, may want the combination plan.

Many employers offer dental plans to their employees, and depending on the cost of the plan, employees may choose to enroll or not. Dental plans now have the same type of choices as medical, either traditional or Dental Managed Organizations (DMOs) or combinations.

Companies may provide group life insurance policies to

employees. The rates on group life insurance are cheaper than individual policies, so even if the employer does not cover the full cost of the premium, it is an inexpensive form of life insurance for an employee. In addition, because most group plans do not require prescreening, many individuals can get coverage they otherwise would not be able to obtain. They normally provide a death benefit as well as coverage for accidents and permanent disabilities. The benefit is usually determined by the employee's position or salary, but if the value of the policy is more than IRS limitations, the additional value is considered taxable income. If employees want additional insurance, or want insurance for spouses or children, these supplemental policies are usually made available by the insurance carrier and the employer, at the employee's cost.

Short- and long-term disability insurance plans are additional benefits that employees value. These disability insurance policies provide income (a percentage of earnings, typically between 50 percent and 67 percent) if an employee becomes unable to work. Short-term disability insurance covers earnings for up to 12 months. Long-term disability insurance begins after the short-term insurance expires. Usually a plan continues for a maximum specified number of months or until the employee turns 65. Either of these plans may require an employee to continue working on a "light duty" basis if the disability allows it.

The range of benefits available to employees today is tremendous, and some employers, especially large ones, may offer all of these plans and let the employee choose. Because one size does not fit all in today's employment environment, one employee may not want to take the family coverage health insurance offered, yet he feels unfairly treated if the company only pays for his single-person coverage. To address this problem, many companies offer cafeteria plans in which a fixed dollar or percentage amount is devoted to benefits, and the employee chooses how to use it. Any contributions made by the employee are governed by Section 125 of the IRS Code, and the amount deducted from pay is considered "pre-tax," reducing the tax bill of the employee.

The most important factors an employer has to consider when deciding which plans to offer its employees are the extent of coverage offered, the quality of the network system, the cost of the insurance premiums, and the amount of administration to be done by the employer. It is critical to read all the offers when shopping for insurance, since a lower premium may mean that the coverage is basic and that certain desirable features are not included; chiropractic or mental health coverage in health insurance, for instance.

Involuntary Benefits: Retirement— Pension Plans, 401(k) Plans, Plans for Small Businesses

Company sponsorship of a retirement plan is purely at the discretion of the employer. However, any company offering a retirement plan to its employees will be governed by the Employee Retirement Income Security Act (ERISA). ERISA serves to protect employee retirement benefits by regulating coverage requirements, eligibility rules, vesting schedules, limits on contributions, limits on benefits, funding requirements, survivor benefits, and termination of plans. Companies use retirement plans, just as they use health insurance and other benefits, to attract and retain good employees. Typically, the contribution to retirement plans is shared between the employer and the employee, or the employee makes contributions that are matched by the employer.

There are various types of retirement plans. Profit-sharing plans designate a portion of the company's profits and add it to the employee's contribution in a trust fund to fund retirement payments. The employer contribution is tied to the employee's salary. Stock-option plans give employees shares in the company or the option to buy shares. 401(k) plans give employees the right to defer a portion of their wages until retirement. Most 401(k) plans include a matching option by the employer, which may be based on length of service. These funds are managed by a brokerage company or investment firm, and the employee decides how his or her funds will be invested. This plan is popular because it places the burden of how to invest pension money in the hands of the employee.

Once an employer has established a retirement plan, he or she must allow all workers who are over the age of 21 and who have worked for the company one year to join.

The requirement is two years if the plan permits 100 percent vesting immediately. Vesting is the employee's right to the pension dollars. Employees are 100 percent vested in any of their own funds they contributed, but may only be vested in the employer portion after a certain length of time, determined by ERISA regulations.

Mike Smith, SPHR
www.mikesmith-hr.com

We employ approximately 2500 people, and we have written job descriptions for each position. All employees have access to the personnel policies, and they know who to contact in the organization should they have any problems, questions, or concerns. In addition, for Internet and phone use, we allow employees reasonable business use and occasional personal use.

We advertise for employees in a number of ways, depending on the position. The Internet and newspapers are valuable recruiting tools. To determine who we will interview, we consider the applicant's résumé. In addition, we do phone screening in relation to job-specific criteria. We don't have any assessment tests; technically, however, the interview process is a test.

> *Mike Smith, SPHR*
> *Six Sigma Certified Black Belt*
> *www.mikesmith-hr.com*

CHAPTER 14

Privacy and Employee Records

I t is important for a company to balance the need to
make employee information available to certain people
in the firm while protecting the employee's right to
privacy regarding this information. Especially today,
when so many records are kept on computer and may
be shared over company intranet systems, controls must
allow access only to employees with a legitimate right
to the information. The management of a company must
also recognize that, despite its need to monitor employee
activity, the employee has certain rights regarding the
surveillance of his or her activities, as discussed in Chapter
7. Publication of private matters, use of an employee's
name or image for commercial purposes without his or
her permission, and disclosure of medical records are

considered an invasion of privacy. In addition, a federal law, the Health Insurance Portability and Accountability Act (HIPAA), specifically protects the medical records of employees.

Surveillance of Employees

Because the Internet and the computers used in a business are the property of the company, judicial decisions have supported the right of the employer to monitor the electronic activity of its employees. This is not necessarily so in the case of phone activity. Because of wire-tapping laws, a company must prove a legitimate business reason to monitor the phone activity of an employee, and it must stop the monitoring if it is clear that the conversation is personal. Controlling the electronic activity is much easier than controlling the phone activity of an employee, and many companies are engaged in the electronic surveillance of their employees to collect data and to monitor any misuse of the computer and the Internet. Because a company can be held liable for the Internet activity of its employees (since it owns and therefore is assumed to control the equipment), many employers require their employees to sign an agreement acknowledging that telephone and Internet communication may be monitored by the company.

Video surveillance of employees is a more sensitive issue. It has been ruled that companies may use video surveillance of employees as long as it is in an office setting. Secret videotaping of employees in such settings as locker rooms, bathrooms, or dressing rooms has been determined to be an invasion of privacy. Senior management of a company must decide where to draw the line regarding the surveillance of its employees. Intrusive monitoring may cause both legal and morale issues that outweigh any benefit obtained by the company. A company must be reasonable in its scope of surveillance and make sure there are legitimate business reasons for it, initiating proper controls to ensure that the privacy of employees is protected. It is not recommended that employers monitor any activity of employees in areas that are considered for the employee's own comfort or for the security of his or her property.

Companies also have the right to search employees, but as a rule, this technique would only be used if the company experiences a high incidence of employee theft. Searches are more common in retail industries than elsewhere. Nonetheless, every employee is entitled to a legitimate expectation of privacy. If desks or lockers are kept locked, and the employee is the only one who has the key, he or she would reasonably be expected to believe that the contents are private, and no one else should have access to them. If, however, the employer maintains and communicates a policy that desks and lockers are the property of the company and may be inspected, the employee would not have an expectation of privacy. The reasonableness of any search in terms of its intrusiveness and necessity may dictate whether the search is an invasion of privacy — or is even legal. In a retail environment where employee shoplifting is a problem, an exit search of employee backpacks, tote bags, or shopping bags might be considered reasonable, especially if the employee is given a locker or other space to keep his or her belongings protected while at work. A body pat-down search, however, would not be considered reasonable.

Drug, Alcohol, and AIDS Testing

Employers are allowed to prohibit drug and alcohol use and possession in the workplace to protect the company and its employees from performance that is impaired by drugs or alcohol. Pre-employment testing for drugs and alcohol is complicated and expensive, but despite the trouble and expense of employee testing, most employers, especially large ones, find it worth the cost. In some industries, in which a lack of sobriety could prove life-threatening, companies may find the cost of not testing much more expensive.

Most companies that require drug testing will have the test administered after a job offer is made. The most common approach is to have the testing done as a condition of employment after the applicant has been hired. If a company decides to do random testing, it has to be extremely careful how it administers such a program to avoid any appearance of discrimination. In these cases, the company is probably better off hiring an outside firm to administer the program so that the choice of those tested will appear truly random. The person administering these tests must be licensed and bonded and comply with certain procedures and notifications, so it is probably best to use certified laboratories. To be in compliance with the law, the tester must:

- Inform the person being tested of his or her rights; that is, that he or she can refuse the test at any time.

- Not ask any questions regarding race, religion, sexual preference, national origin, and so on.

- Maintain a strict chain of custody of the testing sample.

- Not disclose the results of the test to anyone other than the employee and the employer.

If a company decides it wants to do drug and alcohol testing on its current employees, it must be even more careful in the administration of the program. There must be a written policy requiring testing, the employee must have the right to refuse the test and have a grievance procedure in the case of refusal, the testing conditions listed above must be met, and any employee who tests positive must be given the opportunity to enter a rehabilitation program. In the case of testing specific individuals for drugs or alcohol, the employer is taking quite a risk. Unless the problem is presenting a dangerous situation or impairing the employee's performance, such testing is fraught with legal risks. The company must be sure it is warranted. It is difficult to justify such testing, exposing the company to legal actions for invasion of privacy, defamation of character, or wrongful discharge.

Drug and alcohol abusers are protected as a handicapped group under the Americans with Disabilities Act if they are currently in a rehabilitation program and can be certified not to be currently using drugs or alcohol. Current use of alcohol or drugs is not protected under the ADA.

Under the ADA, anyone applying for a job cannot be asked if they have AIDS (Auto Immune Deficiency Syndrome), and cannot be given a test for AIDS unless it is demonstrated that having AIDS is considered "job related and consistent with business necessity," and even then, only if an offer of a job has been made (as discussed previously). However, a Supreme Court decision was handed down in 1987 that limits the refusal of employment to anyone on the basis of a contagious disease based on the severity of the risk, the possible harm to others, and the probability of transmission of the disease to others. Since the Centers for Disease Control and Prevention (CDC) has determined that it is almost impossible to contract AIDS through contact at work, that would make the probability of transmission of the disease very low, and therefore it cannot be used as a basis for refusal of employment. In addition, because having AIDS would not make a person incapable of performing the duties of a job, it cannot be considered "job related and consistent with business necessity" to test him or her. Therefore, in effect, testing for AIDS would, in most cases be considered discriminatory and illegal.

Retention of Records

Employers are required to keep volumes of records regarding their employees. Maintenance of payroll records, health insurance records, and pension records are legally mandated. In addition, for administrative reasons and to protect itself against discrimination cases, a company may want to keep hiring, appraisal, promotion or transfer, discipline, and termination records. In today's complicated legal environment, an employer wants to make sure it has detailed records in case it is brought to court in an employment lawsuit. An employer must be certain that any information gathered and maintained on an employee is protected and used properly.

The retention schedule of certain personnel records is governed by various government legislation and agencies such as the Fair Labor Standard Act (FLSA), the Age Discrimination in Employment Act, the Department of Labor, the Immigration and Naturalization Service, OSHA, and the Internal Revenue Service (IRS). The FLSA requires that employers keep payroll records, separated from the rest of the personnel records, for three years.

The items that must be maintained with the payroll records are all time cards or sheets, W-4s, 941 and 943 records, copies of W-2s, any overtime records, records of commissions or bonuses, and garnishment orders and records. Although there is no set schedule for maintaining other personnel records, active records should be kept for at least three years as well. If any of the records involve ongoing personnel legal actions, they should be held until after the action has been settled.

The IRS requires that I-9 records, which are proof of eligibility to work in the United States, be kept in a separate file for three years after the date of employment, or one year after an employee's termination date, whichever is later. Once an employee leaves the company, his or her files should be maintained in a separate "terminated employee" file so that reference requests from prospective employers can be processed.

ERISA requires that any records related to employee pensions be maintained and these should, at the very least, include the authorization from the employee to make a salary deduction for the pension, and the investment choice of the employee in the case of self-directed pension plans. Health insurance records also should be maintained so that it can be evidenced that the employee authorized payroll deductions for the premium, and insurance enrollment forms should be maintained, as well as any signed waivers if the employee opts out of the health insurance plan because of alternate coverage. Post employment physicals or drug tests, workers' compensation records, any doctor's excuse slips for absences, and any medical records related to FMLA leave should also be kept and all of these health-related records should be kept in a separate medical file. Cafeteria plan choices and deductions should also be documented and retained. The applications, résumés, test scores, and copies of rejection letters for applicants not hired should be retained for one year in compliance with the Age Discrimination in Employment Act. OSHA requires that medical records for employees exposed to toxic substances be retained for 30 years after termination of the employee.

After complying with the laws regarding such records as payroll records, health insurance records, and pension records that must be maintained for each employee, what other kinds of records is it desirable for an employer to maintain on each employee? Information kept in an employee's personnel file should be only information that is job related. An employer may want to keep a linear history of each employee so that an application and résumé, interview records, references, tests taken, a copy of an offer letter, training, development or commendation records, appraisals, promotion or transfer records, salary history records, discipline records, and finally termination and unemployment records, including letters of resignation or layoff notices, would all become a part of the employee's personnel file. However, each of these records serves a specific purpose, and it should not be necessary to allow these records to be viewed by anyone in the company unless there is a legitimate reason.

Interview notes that touch on any aspect of the employee that is not related to his or her qualifications for the job should not be in the file; credit reports obtained should only be used to determine the applicant's trustworthiness — information regarding their personal credit card history should not be part of the records. Personnel files should be kept locked, and any that are in computer records should be password protected.

Computer human resource information systems have made the job of managing employee information easier, but it has also made it necessary to add a new layer of privacy protection. Just as employee files should not be allowed to leave the human resource department and should be viewed in the presence of an HR staff person, computer records should not be carelessly viewed on a computer screen for others to see, and records should not be copied onto discs left for others to view. If an employee file is out of the locked file because records are being added or copies being made, it should be returned immediately and not left around for others to view. If documents intended for an employee file cannot be filed immediately, they should be kept under lock until the filing can take place.

Who Can Access Employee Records?

The employer may want to limit access to information to need-to-know basis. For example, if a supervisor is considering an employee's application for transfer to his department, he should be allowed to view his résumé, training records, attendance records, and appraisals to discover if he or she is a viable candidate for the position. There is no need, however, for that supervisor to view the medical records of the employee. The cleanest way to handle this is to maintain separate subsections in each file. Anything medically related, including disability records, copies of health insurance applications and physicals, and so forth should be kept in a separate folder. This common sense approach now is also required by federal law and the confidentiality of medical records is protected by the Americans with Disabilities Act (ADA). The only people who can be given access to an employee's medical records are a supervisor if he needs to be assured that the employee has no physical limitations (that could not be reasonably accommodated) that would disqualify the employee from the job, medical personnel if they need the information to assist the employee in case of an emergency, and government personnel requiring information regarding compliance with ADA.

Performance-related documents, including results of skills tests, appraisals, and development plans should be kept in a separate folder so that a supervisor can be given this information only. What about an employee's right to view his or her own records? Access to an employee's records may be regulated by state law. Some states require the company to make the records available for inspection by the employee at a reasonable interval (for example, once a year). The employer may coordinate this with the appraisal process, so that the employee can review previous appraisals, note trainings he or she has had, and view any warnings or other disciplinary actions, in preparation for his or her appraisal interview. The company has the right both to expect the employee to read this file on his or her own time, not company time, and to require that a company official be present to ensure the records are not tampered with. The employer may screen the records before this inspection, but the only records that may be removed are references or other information that would violate the privacy of another individual. An employee has the right both to request that erroneous information be removed and to add an explanation to any document with which he or she disagrees. Most states will allow employees to make copies of their records, although the employer may charge a reasonable fee for these copies.

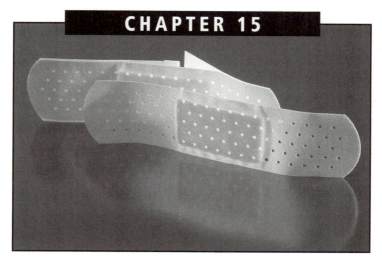

CHAPTER 15

Employee Safety and Health

I t is just good business to protect employees. Injuries and illnesses cost money, slow or stop production, and damage employee morale. Injury and illness can cause untold suffering to families as well as to the employees themselves. In addition, they can often be the cause of damaging lawsuits. Fair, sensible, and well-managed companies automatically make the safety of their employees a top priority. For those companies that do not, or to further guide the efforts of those that do, Congress passed the Occupational Safety and Health Act (OSHA) in 1970 to "assure so far as possible every working man and woman in the nation safe and healthful working conditions and to preserve our human resources." The only employers who are not subject to OSHA regulations are self-employed people, farms in which only family members work, and state and local governments, which are covered by other statutes.

OSHA

The Occupational Safety and Health Administration, which administers the Occupational Safety and Health Act, is an arm of the Department of Labor. The purpose of this administration is to establish and enforce safety and health standards in the United States. OSHA has offices throughout the country with inspectors who monitor most businesses to ensure compliance with the Act. The general safety and health standard that governs OSHA is that each employer should provide a workplace that is free from hazards that may cause death or serious harm to employees. The individual standards are contained in five huge volumes that cover general industry, the construction industry, and the maritime industry as well as regulations and procedures and a field operations manual.

Any company with 11 or more employees must report and maintain records of any occupational injury or illness. An occupational injury is caused by equipment or conditions in the workplace and requires more serious treatment than first aid; an occupational illness is an illness caused by environmental factors associated with employment. (This is a general statement; the OSHA regulations regarding what must be reported as an occupational injury or illness is lengthy and quite specific.) OSHA also regulates what kind of equipment should be used to prevent injury or illness in the workplace such as hard hats or protective footgear on construction sites, safety masks when exposed to gases or fumes, lifting belts for certain tasks, proper scaffolding, machine guards, and so on are all examples of OSHA-required protection.

OSHA requires that the general work environment be safe, meaning that it should not have obstructions to passage, it must have good lighting and ventilation, all equipment must be free from defect and functioning properly, personal protective equipment must be worn in certain circumstances, hazardous materials must be properly labeled and Material Safety Data Sheets provided.

OSHA does not conduct inspections unless they are warranted or an employer requests one as part of a safety improvement program. An OSHA inspection will be warranted if an accident occurs or if there is a valid employee complaint of an unsafe condition or a violation of an OSHA standard. Obviously, OSHA cannot inspect every place of employment where an accident occurs, so certain situations will receive priority. Catastrophes or other such accidents that cause multiple injuries, accidents that cause death, or situations that are viewed as liable to cause either of these are given top priority. If an employee complaint is received, the level of seriousness will determine OSHA's reaction to it. Typically, their first step would be a letter to the employer requesting corrective action in the case of a nonserious situation. If an inspection is required, an OSHA inspector may issue a citation for violations, usually requiring compliance within a certain period. Noncompliance can result in sizeable financial penalties as well as day-by-day fines for the period the employer remains in noncompliance. Usually, working with OSHA to demonstrate willingness to comply, even when full compliance is not possible immediately, will work to reduce penalties.

In attempting to comply with OSHA regulations, employers often encounter employee resistance. Despite the law, many construction workers refuse to wear their hard hats; many electrical workers refuse to use lockout systems. Whether this lack of cooperation stems from attitude, laziness, or time constraints, it is the employer who is held liable for the penalties if the employees refuse to comply with the regulations. A company must initiate and enforce its own safety programs to make sure that its employees are not unwittingly exposing the employer to OSHA violations. Involving the employees in the design of safety programs will aid in these attempts.

Maintaining a Safe Environment

"An ounce of prevention is worth a pound of cure" is the perfect maxim for maintaining employee safety. Management must make a serious commitment to maintaining a safe work environment. In addition, the commitment to safety must be well-communicated. The safety compliance officer, especially in a large company, should be a senior officer. Safety measures and procedures should be a part of senior-level discussions and meetings.

A safety policy should be an integral part of the employee handbook. Short- and long-range corporate goals should include specific measurements for decreasing accidents and safety violation levels. All of these will send a clear message to employees that safety is a top priority in the company.

The first aspects of a safe environment that should be analyzed are the day-to-day operations of a company. These so-called housekeeping issues are the easiest to address, help to set visible standards for safety in general, and are frequently the cause of most serious accidents. They apply in all working environments, not just hard hat or blue-collar environments. Corridors, halls, and stairways should be well lit and slip-proof; all work areas should be free of obstacles; and parts, tools, and supplies should be safely stored between uses. Flooring should be kept clean and dry and free of cracks or breaks that may cause trips and falls. Electrical or communication lines should be installed properly, not strung across floors. Wastebaskets should be located throughout, and emptied frequently. Fire extinguishers or other fire-fighting equipment should be clearly labeled and readily available. A safety officer should be charged with frequent inspections to make sure that the general environment is not encumbered by anything that may invite accidents.

Industry-specific safety measures are usually dictated by the type of work done and the type of equipment used. Most machinery and equipment come with a list of standard maintenance procedures and safety techniques to be used. Keeping equipment properly lubricated; keeping parts in good repair; keeping belts, chains, hooks, and the like safely maintained and secured; using protective covers where necessary; and so on are all steps that will be outlined by the equipment handbook. Proper safety equipment for the operators of machinery and equipment also will be outlined by the manufacturer of the equipment. Following these recommendations and procedures should be mandatory for all operators. Safety manuals should be read, understood, and complied with by all who use the tools or equipment. Many companies will design a safety checklist based on the instructions in the manufacturer's manual to make sure the proper steps are consistently taken to ensure safe operation. Demonstration of safe operation of any such equipment should be part of the job orientation.

In addition to making sure that a work environment is safe for its employees, a company should make sure that its employees act in a safe manner. One landscape materials company was shocked to learn that many of their yard accidents happened because some of the drivers were attempting to do "wheelies" in the front loaders. No amount of brake inspections or lift lubrication is going to prevent those kinds of accidents. Once again, the emphasis on safe behavior must come from senior management. One would think that employees would not need incentives to behave safely, given the fact that they are the ones who will suffer the consequences of unsafe behavior, but ego and the desire to be funny or well liked may cause some employees to take risks. Other unsafe actions may be influenced by laziness or undue speed in completing a task. When employees are given awards for safe behavior, and departments share bonuses for periods without accidents, unsafe behaviors and techniques have been seen to be reduced.

Employee Health Issues: Alcohol, Drugs, Job Stress, Smoking, and Job-Related Injuries

Alcohol and drug abuse are serious workplace issues. In addition to the damage caused to the individual abuser, substance abuse can be the cause of dangerous accidents, a decline in productivity, and the cause of lower morale in the company. Alcohol or drug abusers are frequently problem employees who are difficult for others to work with. Recognizing on-the-job alcohol or drug use is difficult since most supervisors are not counselors trained to work with these problems. In addition, most serious abusers have finely tuned defense mechanisms in place to cover their actions. However, the behavior of substance abusers frequently exhibits in similar ways, and most of these are of concern to management because of the safety, productivity, and morale issues discussed above. Substance abusers are frequently absent, late for work, distracted, or tired while on the job. They may be undependable, causing missed deadlines, errors, and belligerent behavior. Because drug use is an expensive habit to maintain, drug abusers may become frequent borrowers or even thieves. If a supervisor does suspect drug or alcohol abuse, he or she should try to confirm it and make a note of it. Each subsequent instance should be documented with a written warning, and the employee must be told that the next warning will result in referral to the human resource department or employee assistance program.

Given the complications of dealing with substance abusers, most employers would rather not hire them at all and so resort to testing, especially for drug use (see Chapter 14). If a current employee tests positive for alcohol or drug abuse, each company has its own solutions to solving the problem. Some firms have a zero-tolerance policy and will terminate an employee immediately. Most firms use a graduated discipline, such as offering counseling on a first offense, rehabilitation on a second offense, and termination if there are three offenses. An employee can refuse the treatment, but in that case, he can be terminated immediately. An employee who refuses to take a drug test has to be provided with a grievance procedure to address the issue. It doesn't mean he cannot be eventually terminated for refusing, but he must be allowed to present his case for refusal.

The Drug-Free Workplace Act requires employers working under federal contracts or grants to maintain a drug-free workplace and be able to certify that they have taken steps to ensure it. Many companies have used these guidelines in formulating their own drug-free workplace policies and have been able to use them to educate and discipline employees when an issue of substance abuse arises. The federal act requires that employers publish a policy prohibiting the use, possession, or distribution of controlled substances in the workplace; establish an awareness program warning employees of the dangers of substance abuse in the workplace; and inform employees that they have the obligation not only to abide by the policy, but also to report any criminal conviction for drug-related activities in the workplace.

Job stress is fast becoming another workplace problem that is causing illness and injury, as well as lost productivity and low employee morale. Many times, it is job stress that is responsible for alcohol and drug abuse. Work schedules, combined with busy family activities, stressful commutes, lack of job security, and frequent job moves are many of the factors the make modern work life more stressful. Some job stress is to be expected, but an environment of unrelenting stress is extremely unhealthy. Most jobs have peak periods during which the pressure is great, but as long as these times are balanced with periods where the workload is more paced, there should be no long-term consequences. Tax accountants, for example, are accustomed to working long hours between January and April of each year. CPA firms with busy tax departments have found such de-stressing mechanisms as shorter work weeks in the weeks immediately following tax season or parties or outings to release the pressure. Some individuals are more prone to job stress, others thrive on it, and some people can adjust to one type of job stress but not another type.

Short-term stress like that of completing a project by a deadline actually increases some employees' productivity because of the way it forces them to focus. Nonetheless, the consequences of serious job stress can be damaging to both the company and the employee. In fact, there are extremely serious consequences that can even be considered work-related illness, including depression and heart disease. For this reason, most companies work to find methods to relieve stress among their employees. Some of the methods companies use to offer a better work-life balance are discussed in Chapter 12. Flextime, telecommuting, and shared jobs may relieve some of the stress of balancing home responsibilities with work responsibilities. Soliciting feedback from employees and keeping lines of communication open so that employees are free to discuss the stresses of their jobs also have been cited as ways to ease stress. Feeling stressed and then keeping it bottled up only exacerbates the problem. Giving employees more control over their jobs is also a major stress-buster. One of the leading causes of stress in any life situation is a sense of lack of control. Involving employees in decision-making teams, keeping employees informed about product successes and failures, and encouraging employees to feel a part of the "big picture" will give them a sense of control over their destinies, thereby reducing stress.

Since the number of employees who spend most of their time at a computer terminal has grown in recent years, so has the number of health problems related to this type of work. Such problems as eye irritation and stress, back and neck problems, and such "cumulative motion disorders" as carpal tunnel syndrome are more and more common. These problems, illnesses, and disorders have been deemed to be eligible for workers' compensation coverage if they are proven to be job-related. A company can minimize employee exposure to these problems by using certain protective measures and common-sense procedures. Wrist pads; ergonomically designed chairs; terminal screen hoods; and proper positioning of computer, mouse, and keyboard all work to reduce, and, in some cases, eliminate many of the problems that computer operators encounter. Simply taking some time away from repetitive tasks (the National Institute for Occupational Safety and Health, NIOSH, recommends a 15-minute rest break after each 2 hours of work), making sure employees have eye exams and proper corrective lenses, and allowing for work stations to be adjustable to suit each worker will help to relieve the physical strain of working at a computer terminal.

Smoke-Free Workplace

Smoking is another difficult issue for both employer and employee. Luckily for some employers, recent legislation banning smoking has shifted the burden of enforcing no-smoking policies from the company to the government. Most companies recognize the cost of smoking but have had a tough time balancing the rights of smokers with the needs of the nonsmokers and of the company. Smokers cost a company more in terms of health costs, lost time (to smoking breaks), absenteeism, and fire risks. Studies have even shown that smokers have a greater risk of work-related accidents than nonsmokers ("Where There's Smoke

There's Risk," BNA *Bulletin to Management*, January 30, 1992, pp. 26, 31.) Although a compassionate company may be concerned about the risk to an employee's health from smoking, factors such as accidents and lost productivity are a driving force behind an effort to eliminate smoking in the workplace. In addition, nonsmokers who feel threatened by inhaling second-hand smoke have started to sue their employers who do not protect them from this smoke on the grounds that OSHA requires them to provide a reasonably safe workplace.

Violence in the Workplace

Violence against employees is a major problem in the workplace. Robbery is the primary motive for workplace homicide in 85 percent of the cases, but a co-worker or personal associate committed roughly one of seven workplace homicides, according to Gus Toscano and Janaice Windau in "The Changing Character of Fatal Work Injuries," *Monthly Labor Review*, October, 1994. While most violence in the workplace does not escalate to the level of murder, there is a growing concern over danger to workers. Maintaining a safe environment will help by improving lighting, using surveillance cameras, limiting access to strangers, installing silent alarms, and other measures, but eliminating a problem within, such as employee-against-employee violence, is more difficult. A company must screen out potentially violent individuals from employment in the first place through their referral and reference process. All companies should have a ban against weapons in the workplace. All employees, especially supervisors, should be trained to recognize behavior that may escalate to violence and to implement measures to take in the face of such behavior. Threats, veiled or otherwise; actions intended to intimidate others; or any kind of obsession, including an unsolicited romantic stalking behavior are serious warning signs. In addition, evidence of drug or alcohol abuse and erratic mood swings should alert management. The company cannot choose to ignore such behavior. A member of management, preferably someone from the human resource department, should discuss any threatening behavior or words with the employee. Let the employee know that this behavior is not acceptable, but let him have the opportunity to discuss his problem through the employee assistance plan or through outside counseling. A company with a culture that fosters respect, civil behavior, and sensitivity will have less of a problem with employee violence than one that allows its employees to feel marginalized. A number of cases in which a terminated employee or one who was passed over for a promotion became violent might have been avoided if the situation had been handled more sensitively.

If, despite all efforts, a violent action does take place, a company should have an emergency procedure in place to react to it, counseling resources for any victims, and a safety plan for return to work.

Ken Patterson Sr.
ASM/EMT/PSM/CSSO

We try to offer employees the safest work environment possible; to ensure safety, we have a VPP worksite, job site audits, facility audits, and required safety meetings.

Because we are a very large company, we have a lot of opportunity for advancement. We keep our employees informed of job openings and other company news through e-mail and newsletters. It's also important to receive employee feedback, which we encourage through an open-door policy, suggestions boxes, and open forums which the president conducts.

Annually, we conduct a performance appraisal on all employees, which consists of a grading score sheet for non represented employees. For employees who go above and beyond their required duties, the company awards the Golden Achiever Award.

CHAPTER 16

Labor Relations and Collective Bargaining

I n a unionized company, conditions of employment, wage levels, pensions, and other such issues are agreed upon by formal bargaining between the management of the company and the representatives of the union. Companies are prohibited from discriminating against workers on the basis of union membership or activity. So even if a company does not have a union now, union representatives may try to work with employees to unionize a company. Most companies would rather negotiate directly with their employees rather than have them represented by a union, but many people believe they would be better represented by union leaders who are more familiar with labor laws and practices. Of course, there is apparent strength in numbers. Despite the fact that companies do not want their employees to be represented by a union, employers have to be careful not to violate the laws pertaining to unions by threatening employees with the loss of their jobs if they join.

Even in companies and industries in which the employees are not represented by unions, unions may still have a great impact because of their bargaining powers over employee wage levels and such benefits as sick days, vacation days, and pension agreements. Frequently, union agreements become a benchmark employees use to judge how fair their pay or benefits are.

Unions and Employment Law

A number of national legislative acts, including the Norris-La Guardia Act, the National Labor Relations Act (NLRA), or Wagner Act, and the Taft-Hartley Act cover matters relating to employer-union relations. In general, these laws 1) protect the rights of employees to form and belong to unions, 2) regulate how employers may treat members of unions, and 3) protect the rights of employees in regards to unions.

Employers may not interfere with employees' rights to join or organize unions, and also may not financially support a union. An employer may not discriminate in hiring based on a person's union membership and may not refuse to enter into collective bargaining with a recognized union. The other side of the coin is that unions may not restrain employees in their rights or require employers to discriminate against employees who choose not to join a union. Just as a company may not refuse to bargain with a union, unions may not refuse to bargain with an employer. Unions also are prohibited from charging excessive dues. In other words, the right of a citizen to either join a union or not to join a union is protected. A closed shop is a company that is required to hire only members of the union with which the company has a contract; this arrangement was outlawed by the Taft-Hartley Act. A union shop is a company in which employees must become members of a union; this is allowed by law.

Unions are usually formed in two ways: a group of disgruntled employees decides they cannot get their employer to agree to better wages, benefits, or conditions, and so they invite a union in to represent them. Another scenario is that in which a union targets a company and sends representatives to speak to employees, trying to convince them that the union can get them better wages, benefits, or conditions.

In order for an election for a union to take place, 30 percent of the employees of a company must sign authorization cards. The National Labor Relations Board (NLRB) will conduct a representation election once this number of authorization cards is gathered. Employers may not threaten employees regarding membership in the union, but they are allowed to campaign against union membership, persuading employees of the advantages of remaining union-free. Of course, the union will campaign just as hard to convince the employees that their interests will be best represented by the union.

Collective Bargaining

In a union environment, a company representative will negotiate most aspects of employee relations with a representative of the union. Once a union is certified by the NLRB, it will have the right to represent the employees to the company. Unions are organized on a hierarchical basis, with a national, or even international union, and a "local," which is the basic unit. The officers of the local will conduct meetings and collect dues. A shop steward in each department of a company represents the employees on a day-to-day basis, and a business representative will represent the employees in contract negotiations and compliance.

Collective bargaining is the term for the negotiation that takes place between the representative of a union and the representative of an employer. Typically, a union will try to negotiate a contract with an employer that will call for increased wages, better benefits, and better working conditions. The employer will, in turn, counter with compromises that may save the company money or increase productivity. The company should be familiar with the wage structure in the geographical area as well as in the industry represented and be able to defend its counteroffers with statistics. Union representatives will probably have the demands of their members to represent as well as the success of other unions regarding those demands. Both sides should be clear about requirements, and they should know which bargaining points can be bent and which cannot, as well as which items they are willing to sacrifice in order to obtain others. Depending on the conditions presented on each side, there will be some give and take until an agreement is reached. The negotiators of the contract must pay careful attention to the wording of each clause, making sure they understand both the present and future impact of every point in the contract. The points of negotiation of a union contract are usually wages and automatic increases, hours of work and overtime, requirements for overtime, job security and seniority, benefits such as vacations and holidays, insurance and pensions, disciplinary procedures, health and safety guarantees, and grievance and arbitration procedures.

The union agreement is for a fixed length of time, and when the term of the contract expires, a new negotiation will start. Usually, if the contract is for more than one year, the union will try to put interim wage increases in the contract. Many times, the employer will try to counterbalance wage increases either with reductions in benefits or with higher contributions toward benefits by the employees. These negotiations may take days, and the employees may work without a contract for the interim period. If, after days of negotiations, the union and the employer cannot come to an agreement on all of the terms of the contract, the union will usually use some strong-arm techniques to put pressure on the company to accede.

A strike is the strongest tactic — the company's employees walk off the job and onto picket lines where they vocalize their complaints. The company loses production capabilities, and the employees lose wages. Sometimes, some of the wages are offset by union supplements or unemployment, and the company can continue operating with management or outside help brought in to take over the striking employees' jobs. This is not a situation that can last very long. Frequently, union members will try to stop others from crossing their picket line, and they will also issue boycotts so that members of other unions will not deal with the company and so that the public who sympathize will not buy the company's products. A company can protect itself from some of the negative impacts of a strike by protecting its property and by notifying suppliers and customers that it is working with the union to find a settlement that is fair to both sides. The company may also attempt to gather evidence that picketers are acting illegally. Fair and equitable negotiation of reasonable employee demands through the collective bargaining process is the most sensible route for both the union and the company.

Grievance Procedures

Once the terms of the contract are agreed upon, most of the issues between the employer and the employee will be decided by the grievance procedure. In companies without unions, the employee is usually encouraged to come to an agreement with his supervisor if there are any problems on the job. If that does not work, there is usually protocol in place that allows him to go further up the corporate hierarchy to resolve the dispute. If a union employee has a complaint, he files a grievance through his shop steward, who brings it with the employee to the supervisor. Each contract has its own list of steps in the procedure, some simple two- or three-step procedures and some involving many more steps. If the shop steward and the supervisor come to an agreement, the matter is resolved; if not, the shop steward brings the matter to the next level of management within the company.

At a higher level, the employee may now be represented by the union business representative or a local union official. If an agreement still is not reached, and the grievance goes even further, the human resource manager may represent the company while the chief union official represents the employee. A final level of the grievance procedure is arbitration by a neutral third party. Most union contracts have an arbitration clause that will designate which person or organization will be the arbitrator. The decision made by arbitration is final. Usually a grievance will not go to such a level unless it is a major point of contention, or if it is an issue that may create a precedent, having either a major impact on the company or the employees. Many times, the incident that was the cause of the grievance is beyond resolution. At that time, the company will want to use the grievance procedure to establish a penalty for the issue. Imagine that a union employee wanted to take a personal day and her supervisor denied it because the plant was working to meet a deadline. If no agreement could be reached at the various levels, the employee may have taken her personal day during the proceedings. At that point, the company may want to dock her the day's pay or discipline her in some other way to show (if the company prevailed) that employees did not have the right to take an unapproved personal day.

At every level of the collective bargaining and the grievance processes, both parties, the union and the employer, have an obligation to bargain "in good faith." This means that each must offer solutions and counter proposals and that each must make a valid effort to come to an agreement. In practice, this means that the union's local official cannot completely disregard the company's justification and business necessity of operating within production deadlines solely because he has to represent the employee. The company also must make sure that the decision by the supervisor was not an arbitrary one, but was grounded in sound business needs. Both sides, therefore, must adhere to the NLRB's rules regarding good-faith bargaining. These rules prohibit the sides from going through the motions and not truly bargaining, as well as from exhibiting an unwillingness to make any compromises. They also are prevented from using delaying tactics or changing demands during the negotiations. Neither side may withhold information from the other or from an arbitrator, nor can they bypass the legitimate representative of either side.

A company can avoid or at least reduce the number of

grievances by promoting fair and equitable treatment of employees and by developing a work environment in which problems can be solved before they reach the status of a grievance.

COMPANY: Auxiliary Services Corporation

Michelle K. Brackin, Human Resources Manager

We do not give employees any expectation of privacy when using business technology equipment, including the Internet, except as required by law. Furthermore, we do not conduct drug tests.

We have an active safety committee that reviews safety concerns and solutions used in other departments. We examine annually the accidents from previous years to see if training is needed in an area. When we provide training, we measure the change in those types of accidents.

Unfortunately, we have a severe problem with poor attendance. Employees use all of their sick time as they earn it and take excessive amounts of unpaid time off. Our employees only work the academic year and have several weeks that they are not working to conduct medical or dental appointments or other personal business. We instituted a policy of discipline for any unpaid time that is not approved in advance by a manager. This has curbed the unpaid time off abuse.

Michelle K. Brackin, Human Resources Manager
Auxiliary Services Corporation
Neubig Hall SUNY Cortland • Cortland, NY 13045
Brackinm@cortland.edu • Ascweb.cortland.edu
Phone: 607-753-2431

CHAPTER 17

Performance Problems, Discipline Procedures, and Termination

E ven the best-run companies with the best management teams and best-trained and highly motivated employees still encounter performance problems that need to be addressed. The discipline procedures used to solve some of the problems may range from simple counseling all the way to termination. However, the best way to handle any performance problem is to address it as early as possible.

Addressing Poor Performance

A company should not wait until the first appraisal period

to address any problems observed in a new employee's performance. If a problem is detected, work with the employee as soon as possible to correct the issue. Problem performance does not go away and often will get worse. If an employee doesn't know he is doing his job incorrectly, he will continue to do it the same — wrong — way. Continuing to do it that way will reinforce the behavior. In other words, he will get really good at doing it the wrong way.

Most problems with poor performance stem from poor training. If an employee is having difficulty, first examine whether he has the proper skills to perform the task. Retraining, especially in the case of new employees, may be an easy solution. Be sure the employee understands the goals and standards of the task. Once the poor performance in a specific area has been identified, the employee's supervisor should work closely with him to discover what needs to be done to improve performance. Goals should be set, with timelines attached.

If performance does not improve within a reasonable length of time, the company may have to recognize that the employee simply may not be a good fit. If the job can be adjusted to accommodate the skills of the employee, and if the company is willing to make these accommodations, perhaps some changes can be made to help the employee. The opposite situation also may exist, and an employee may "underperform" because his skills are not challenged.

Personal Problems

Many personal problems, particularly substance abuse as discussed in Chapter 15, can adversely influence job performance. Personal problems may be temporary and have a short-term impact on an employee's ability to function at her peak, or there may be underlying issues that pervade an employee's life. If a personal problem like a divorce, death of a family member, or a temporary financial struggle is affecting an employee's performance, it is wisest for a company to help as much as possible without intruding. This is a delicate area and a difficult challenge, but an employee who survives a difficult period supported by her employer will probably feel a renewed sense of loyalty to her company.

Long-term personal problems that affect job performance pose a completely different challenge. Serious problems related to mental illness or to substance abuse must be left to professional counselors. Many companies now contract with an Employee Assistance Program provider to be able to let professionals handle these kinds of problems. When they do work, both the company and the employee will benefit. Unfortunately, there are instances when even intervention by the company or by outside professionals will not alleviate the situation.

Behavior Problems

If, after repeated training, an employee cannot perform

the functions of his job, if he is frequently absent or late, or if he shows performance lapses attributable to drug or alcohol abuse, the management of a company can find easy justification in disciplinary action leading to termination. However, there are many times when an employee performs his job responsibilities with near perfect capability, has good attendance, and meets the general standards of the job requirements, but he is not able to behave civilly to his fellow workers. What should a company do about behavior problems that are not related to poor performance? Should failure to get along with co-workers be considered poor performance in and of itself? The severity of the behavior and the reaction by co-workers should be the first determinants of how management should handle behavior problems. Abusive behavior can be considered harassment and should be dealt with as such. If any comments or behavior by an employee are discriminatory or sexual in nature, the offending employee should be counseled and trained in those aspects of employment law. Disciplinary action must follow if such comments or behavior continues. Surliness and poor attitude toward supervisors can be considered insubordination, which also can require discipline. But what about the quiet, shy worker who just does his job and doesn't want to socialize much? His behavior can be considered problem behavior because communication is so critical in today's working world. As any performance in a work environment can be improved by proper training, employees can be trained in personal relations that will lead to better cooperation among workers.

Discipline

Once a company has a good personnel policy in place to train employees, monitor performance of their duties, and prevent problems and behaviors that will impede the overall performance of the company, everything should go smoothly, right? Of course not. No matter how good a company's policies are and how closely they are followed, there will still be performance problems that require attention.

In most companies, the concept of progressive discipline is followed. It is important to be careful when using the term progressive discipline, since it can imply that if the next step in the discipline process is not necessary, then the employee has "passed the test" and now cannot be fired.

Progressive discipline was designed to give an employee a chance to recognize that his performance or behavior needs to be improved and to provide employers with a trail indicating that efforts were made to correct poor performance or behavior. The levels of progress of the discipline differ, but most of the time, a company will issue an oral warning and two written warnings. The second written warning will advise the employee that he will be terminated if the behavior continues or if the performance does not improve. Each level of warning should be accompanied by offers of assistance to resolve the problem. Even if an oral warning is given, notes should be taken documenting the discussion. All warnings should be given in a clear, professional manner, without any personal incrimination: "Our company policy prohibits the use of alcohol or drugs during working hours," not "You're a drunk!" Each level of discipline should give the employee an opportunity to appeal the warning, but the company should be careful not to turn the procedure into a battle. The employee needs to follow the regulations and perform his responsibilities; continued excuses cannot be tolerated.

Grounds for Dismissal

The usual grounds for dismissal are unsatisfactory job performance, misconduct, lack of qualification for the position, and elimination of the position (layoff). If, after sufficient efforts to retrain and reinforce good job performance, the company finds that an employee cannot perform the job to the standards required, it is justified in dismissing him for unsatisfactory job performance. Performing according to the standards may not mean only that he is unable to produce 50 widgets a week. It may also mean that he is consistently late and frequently absent, which, of course, will lead to not being able to produce 50 widgets a week.

Misconduct is the deliberate violation of a company's rules. Harassment, stealing, drinking, or gambling on the job will result in dismissal for misconduct. Lack of qualification for the position is basically an admission that the wrong employee was hired for the position. Most of the time, once a company makes the commitment to hire a person, and that person is cooperating in attempting to perform the job, the company will make every effort to assist him. A transfer may even be considered. If the company is downsizing, a job may be eliminated and staff let go. If an employee is dismissed for job performance, misconduct, or lack of qualifications, the company should make every effort to make sure the dismissal is viewed as fair. This is important not only because of issues of wrongful discharge suits but also because other employees need to feel that they will not lose their jobs simply at the whim of the boss.

Terminating an Employee Legally, Tactfully, and Ethically

Once the management of a company has decided that an employee should be terminated because of poor performance or behavior problems, the supervisor should do his or her utmost to protect the dignity and rights of the employee. Other than terminations or layoffs that are part of a downsizing or seasonal business cycles, most terminations for cause are tricky and emotionally charged on both sides. The employee, of course, is emotionally affected, but often the supervisor may be annoyed and frustrated with the employee. Employers have to be careful that the causes for termination are valid and have been documented. Even where a company claims it has a "termination at will" policy, there have been cases in which an employee may consider his termination wrongful and will file a lawsuit.

Properly handling the termination of an employee will help avoid these lawsuits. People who feel embarrassed, treated unfairly, or stripped of their dignity are more likely to pursue recourse than those who believe they were given a fair chance and then let go with their dignity intact. Carefully following discipline procedures will make the process easier, since the employee will have received three or four opportunities to correct the problem. Usually, the decision to terminate will be made by a team of people that includes the human resource manager, or even the president in a smaller company. This approach is wise, since each discipline document should be reviewed to be sure the employee was treated fairly and that there are no grounds for discrimination charges.

Once the decision has been made, the termination should be carried out quickly. Even if the employer is obligated or decides to give notice, it is best to just pay the salary for the notice period and allow the employee to leave the premises. A "lame duck" employee can do untold harm if he continues to work, both in terms of work produced and the impact he can have on morale. Since the situation may have become emotionally charged, it may be best if a neutral party such as the HR manager, instead of the employee's supervisor, carry out the termination. Preparing for the termination interview in advance will allow both the HR department and the supervisor to choose their words and actions carefully, allowing the employee to maintain his dignity throughout the procedure. They should also be prepared for a violent reaction and have a game plan in mind.

The Termination Interview

Preparing for a termination interview involves a number of things. An appointment should be set, and the interviewer should not be cajoled into telling the employee over the phone. An employee who has had a number of warnings and then is told he needs to attend a meeting with the supervisor may have a strong suspicion about the purpose of the meeting. Nevertheless, the person handling the interview needs to stand his ground; the termination itself is only a part of the interview. The interview should be held in a neutral, private place. The person handling the termination should have available any relevant documentation, including warnings and personnel policy. He should be polite, but to the point — this is not the time for small talk. Use neutral language like "the company requires 500 entries per hour, and despite repeated trainings, you are producing only 300." He should avoid recriminations, but also not excuse the policy of the company. He should just stick to the facts at hand and remain professional.

The interview should not last longer than ten minutes. The employee should be allowed time to respond or ask questions regarding the termination, as long as he is calm and understands the situation. The interviewer should be prepared in the event of a violent reaction and should have phone numbers ready for medical or security personnel. The next step in the procedure should be explained, as well as what is expected of the employee. "Joe will walk you to your desk and help with your personal belongings.

We request that you leave the building immediately after that." If the supervisor and HR department have been as discreet as they should have been, and if there has been no gossip by the employee or others, the termination should take place with little disruption. If it is handled smoothly and tactfully, the employee will have left before the rumor mills even get started. The company should have an announcement regarding the situation prepared in advance. If the employee wants to keep in contact with his associates, that is his business. The company should not tell employees they should not talk to the dismissed employee.

Severance Pay and Termination Benefits

At the termination interview, the employee should receive all documentation and information relevant to his termination. These will include:

- Unemployment forms and booklets, if applicable.

- Forms for continued health insurance benefits under C.O.B.R.A.

- Amount of severance pay (including sick and vacation days that may be payable) and how and when it will be paid, plus any outstanding reimbursements due.

- How pension or other retirement benefits will be

affected and who to contact regarding them.

- Who to contact at the company for assistance or support.

- What kind of outplacement services are available.

- Who is responsible for employment reference information.

The interviewer should be sure to secure any property of the company's that the employee may have. A list should be prepared ahead of time of any property that has been signed out by the employee, including laptops, cell phones, corporate credit cards, keys, and access cards. If any property of the company is at the home of the employee, such as a computer, arrangements should be made to recover it. Remind the employee of any confidentiality or proprietary agreements he has agreed to and let him know that passwords or access codes will be cancelled. It is also a good idea at this time to verify the terminated employee's correct address.

CHAPTER 18

Conclusion

All of this illustrates that, in any business, large or small, knowing the basics of human resource management will help a company toward success. In most industries, especially the knowledge fields, the human resource aspect is often 90 percent of the corporate budget. Hiring a professional manager to oversee the human resource function in a company is usually the best solution. However, even for small businesses, the complexities of government requirements, laws, taxes, legal aspects, and the threat of suits related to employment matters are important issues that every businessperson must be aware of. The company or owner of the company has to decide whether a personnel policy should be developed and, if so, what it should contain. Based on manpower needs, the company head has to decide who to hire and how to recruit and hire them, and has to make sure all the steps in the hiring process are fair and legal and that these steps will bring the best employees on board.

Once an employee is hired, a human resource manager's or company owner's job is far from over. Training, motivating, and retaining employees and making sure that employees are fairly compensated and are all given the opportunity to advance in the company are an integral part of managing human resources. As an employer, keeping employees safe and providing benefits for them and their families becomes an integral part of the employer-employee relationship.

How does the company ensure this? Continual education in resources such as this, which educate human resource managers in all of the issues surrounding personnel matters, is the best way to make sure that a company not only succeeds but thrives.

CHAPTER 19

Resources

Aguanno, Kevin, *101 Ways to Reward Team Members for $20 (or Less!)*, Multi-Media Publications Inc., Lakefield, Ontario, 2004.

Dessler, Gary, *Human Resource Management*, 9th edition, Prentice Hall, New Jersey, 2003.

Fein, Richard, *101 Hiring Mistakes Employers Make and How to Avoid Them*, Impact Publications, Virginia, 2000.

Hannay, Maureen and Melissa Northam, "Low-Cost Strategies for Employee Retention," *Compensation and Benefits Review*, July-August 2000, pp 66-72.

Joel, Lewin G. III, *Every Employee's Guide to the Law: What You Need to Know About Your Rights in the Workplace — and What to Do if They Are Violated*, 3rd ed, rev. ed, Pantheon Books, New York, 1996.

Messmer, Max, *Human Resources Kit for Dummies*, IDG Books Worldwide, Inc., California, 1999.

Pell, Dr. Arthur R., *The Complete Idiot's Guide to Human Resource Management*, Alpha Books, Indiana, 2001.

Shawn A. Smith and Rebecca A. Mazin, *The HR Answer Book: An Indispensable Guide for Managers and Human Resources Professionals*, American Management Association, New York, 2004.

Sullivan, William, *Entrepreneur Magazine: Human Resources for Small Businesses*, Wiley, New York, 1997.

Toscano, Gus and Janice Windau, "The Changing Character of Workplace Injuries," *Monthly Labor Review*, October, 1994.

Truss, Catherine and Lynda Gratton, "Strategic Human Resource Management: A Conceptual Approach," *International Journal of Human Resource Management*, Sept. 1994, v5, n3, pp 663 (24).

"Where There's Smoke There's Risk," *BNA Bulletin to Management*, January 30, 1992, p. 26, 31.

Glossary

360-Degree Feedback
A method in which an employee may receive feedback on their own performance from their supervisor and up to eight co-workers, reporting staff members, or customers.

A

Absence or Absent (Scheduled) A period of time off from work that is previously planned during a normally scheduled work period.

Absence or Absent (Unscheduled) A period of time off from work during a normally scheduled work period that has not been planned.

Absenteeism Policy
A policy that provides guidance within an organization regarding managing an employee's chronic absence from work.

Absorptive Capacity The ability of a company to identify, value, assimilate, and use newly acquired knowledge.

Acquisitions The strategy a company uses to enter a new business area and develop it by buying an existing business.

Adaptive Cultures The environment within a company where employees, who are innovative, are encouraged, and initiative is awarded by middle- and lower-level managers.

Attendance Policy The expectations and guidelines for employees to report to work as written, distributed, and enforced by an organization.

B

Background Checking The act of looking into a person's employment, security, or financial history before offering employment or granting a license.

Behavioral Interview An analysis of answers to situational questions that attempts to determine if you have the behavioral characteristics that have been selected as necessary for success in a particular job.

Benefits Additions to employees' base salary, such as health insurance, dental insurance, life insurance, disability insurance, a severance package, or tuition assistance.

Bereavement Policy The portion of an employment contract that provides for a certain amount of time off from work when an employee's spouse or close family member passes away.

Bonus Plan A system of rewards that generally recognizes the performance of a company's key individuals, according to a specified measure of performance.

Bottom-Up Change A gradual process in which

the top management in a company consults with several levels of managers in the organization and develops a detailed plan for change with a timetable of events and stages the company will go through.

Broadbanding A salary structure in which pay ranges are consolidated into broader categories to reduce overlap with other pay ranges.

C

Capabilities The skills a company has in coordinating its resources efficiently and productively.

Cash Flow The amount of cash a business receives minus cash that must be distributed for expenses.

Centralization A type of hierarchy in an organization in which upper-level managers have the authority to make the most important decisions.

Clarity of Expectations The concept that before, during, and after strategic decisions are made, managers should have a clear understanding of what is expected of them, as well as an idea of any new rules or strategies.

Coaching A method used by managers and supervisors for providing constructive feedback to employees in order to help them continue to perform well, or to identify ways in which they can improve their performance.

Cognitive Bias Errors in the methods human decision makers use to process information and reach decisions.

Commission System A system of rewards in which

employees are paid based on how much they sell.

Company Infrastructure A work environment in which all activities take place, including the organizational structure, control systems, and culture.

Conflict Aftermath The long-term effects that emerge in the last stage of the conflict process.

Congruence The state in which a company's strategy, structure, and controls work together.

Corporate Governance The strategies used to watch over managers and ensure that the actions they take are consistent with the interests of primary stakeholders.

Counseling The act of providing daily feedback to employees regarding areas in which their work

performance can improve.

Cycle An iteration of the planning process which begins with the corporate mission statement and major corporate goals.

D

Decentralization An organizational hierarchy in which authority has been delegated to divisions, functions, managers, and workers at lower levels in the company.

Devil's Advocacy A way of improving decision making by generating a plan and a critical analysis of that plan.

Dialectic Inquiry A way to improve decision making by generating a plan and a counter-plan.

Differentiation The method a company uses to allocate people and resources to certain tasks in the organization to create value.

Discipline A process of dealing with job-related behavior that does not meet communicated performance expectations.

Diversification The process of entering into new industries or business areas.

Division The portion of a company that operates in a particular business area.

Downsizing The process of reducing the employees headcount in an organization.

Dress Code for Business Casual A company's objective to enable employees to project a professional, business-like image while experiencing the advantages of more casual and relaxed clothing.

E

Efficiency The measurement derived from dividing output by input.

Emotional Intelligence A term that describes a bundle of psychological characteristics that many strong leaders exhibit (self-awareness, self-regulation, motivation, empathy, and social skills).

Empathy The psychological characteristic that refers to understanding the feelings and viewpoints of subordinates and taking them into account when making decisions.

Employee Empowerment The process of enabling or authorizing an individual to think, behave, take action, and control work and decision-making autonomously.

Employee Involvement The act of creating an environment in which people may take part in decisions or actions that affect their jobs.

Employee Stock Option Plan (ESOP) A system of rewarding employees in which they may buy shares in the company at below-market prices.

Employment Eligibility Verification (I-9) The form required by the Department of Homeland Security U.S. Citizenship and Immigration Services to document an employee's eligibility to be employed in America.

Engagement The process of involving individuals in active decision making by asking them for their input and by allowing them to refute the merits of one another's ideas and assumptions.

Exempt Employee Employees who are not confined by the laws governing standard minimum wage and overtime.

Explanation The idea that all those who are involved and/or affected should be told the basic reasoning for strategic decisions and why some ideas and inputs may have been overridden.

F

Fair Labor Standards Act (FLSA) The legislation that requires a company to pay a nonexempt employee who works more than a 40 hour week 150 percent of their regular hourly rate for the overtime hours.

Family and Medical Leave Act (FMLA) The legislation that states that covered companies must grant an eligible employee up to 12 weeks of unpaid leave during any 12-month period of time for one or more of the covered reasons.

Feedback The information given to or received from another person regarding the impact of their actions on a person, situation, or activity.

Felt Conflict The type of conflict occurring at the stage in which managers start to personalize the disagreement.

Franchising A business strategy in which the franchisor grants the franchisee the right to use the parent company's name, reputation, and business skills at a particular location or area.

Functional Structure An organizational method of grouping people based on their common expertise and experience or on the same set of resources those people use.

G

Garnishment A legal procedure in which a person's earnings are withheld by an employer for the repayment of a debt.

General Manager A person who bears all responsibility for the organization's overall performance or that of one of its major self-contained divisions.

Goal The future state a company attempts to reach.

H

Horizontal Differentiation The way in which the company focuses on the grouping of people and tasks into functions and divisions to meet the objectives of the business.

Human Resources (1) The people who are part of an organization and its operations. (2) The business function that deals with the employees of a company.

Independent Contractor A person or a business that performs services or supplies a product for a person or a business under a written or implied contract.

Industry A group of companies that offer products or services that are similar to each other.

Integration The process by which a company coordinates people and functions to accomplish certain tasks within the organization.

Internal Governance The way in which the top executives in a company manage individuals within the organization.

J

Job Offer Letter A written document that confirms the details of an offer of employment, including details such as the job description, reporting relationship, salary, bonus potential, and benefits.

L

Labor-Management Glossary A comprehensive list of the definitions of labor management terms provided by the U.S. Office of Personnel Management.

Learning Effects The cost savings that come from learning while performing the task.

Legitimate Power The authority a manager holds due to being placed in a formal position in the organization's hierarchy.

M

Management by Objectives (MBO) A process in which managers participate in their evaluation of their capability to achieve certain organizational goals or performance standards and to meet the given operating budget.

Marketing Strategy The stand a company takes regarding pricing, promotion, advertising, product design, and distribution.

Minimum Wage The minimum amount of compensation per hour for covered, nonexempt employees as defined by the Fair Labor Standards Act (FLSA) and by local states.

Mission Statement A brief but precise definition of what an organization does and why.

Motivation A psychological portion of emotional intelligence that refers to a passion for work that goes beyond money or status and enables a person to pursue goals with energy and persistence.

N

Negativity The concept and expression of unhappiness, anger, or frustration to other employees in the workplace.

Networking The act of building interpersonal relationships that could be mutually beneficial.

New Employee Orientation Also call Induction. The process of orienting a new employee to a company, usually performed by one or more representatives from the human resource department.

Non-Exempt Employee Employees who are protected by the laws governing standard wages and overtime.

O

Occupational Outlook Handbook A nationally recognized source of career information that is designed to provide assistance to individuals who are making decisions about their careers.

Operations Manager An individual who is responsible for particular business operations.

Optimism The ability or tendency to look at the positive side of a situation or to expect the best possible results from any series of events.

Organization Bonus System A system of rewards based on the performance measurement of the organization during the most recent time period.

Organizational Politics The strategies that managers use to obtain and use power in order to influence business processes to further their own interests.

Organizational Values Concept regarding the goals that individuals within an organization should pursue and what behavioral standards they should follow to achieve these goals.

Orientation See New Employee Orientation.

Outsourcing The act of paying another individual or business to perform certain internal processes or functions.

P

Perceived Conflict Conflict that occurs when managers are made aware of clashes within an organization.

Performance Management A policy for dealing with behavior on the job that does not meet expected and communicated performance standards.

Piecework Plan A system of rewards in which output can be accurately measured, and employees are paid based on a set amount.

Profit-Sharing System A system of rewards that compensates employees based on the company's profit during a specified time period.

Progressive Discipline A process for dealing with behavior on the job which does not meet expected and communicated performance standards.

Project Management The process of applying knowledge, skills, tools, and techniques to a wide range of activities in order to meet the requirements of the particular project.

Promotion The act of advancing an employee to a position with a higher salary range maximum.

Q

Quality A measurement of excellence in the desirable

characteristics of a product, a process, or a service.

R

Recognition A practice of providing attention or favorable notice to another person.

Recruiters People who are hired by a company to find and qualify new employees for the organization.

Restructuring A method of improving company performance by reducing the level of differentiation and downsizing the number of employees to decrease operating expenses.

S

Screening Interview A quick, efficient discussion that is used to qualify candidates before they meet with the hiring authority.

Self-Awareness The psychological characteristic of a person's emotional intelligence in which he is able to understand his own moods, emotions, drives, and his effect on others.

Self-Discipline The psychological ability to control one's own behavior.

Self-Regulation The psychological ability to control or redirect one's own disruptive impulses or moods.

Sexual Harassment The act of an employee's making continued, unwelcome sexual advances, requests for sexual favors, and/or other verbal or physical conduct toward another employee against her/his wishes.

Sexual Harassment Investigation The process of looking into an employee's complaint of sexual or other harassment in the workplace.

Social Skills The psychological ability to interact purposefully with others at a friendly level.

Span of Control The number of employees a manager manages directly.

Strategic Control The process in which managers monitor an organization's ongoing activities, members, and correct performance as necessary.

Strategic Control Systems Formal systems for target setting, measurement, and feedback that allow managers to evaluate whether a company is achieving top efficiency, quality, innovation, and customer responsiveness, and implementing its strategy successfully.

Strategic Leadership The charisma of someone that enables him to articulate a strategic vision for the company or part of the company and motivates others to share that vision.

Strategic Management Process The process in which a set of goals or strategies is chosen by managers for the enterprise.

T

Top-Down Change An adjustment that occurs when a strong upper-management team analyzes how to alter strategy and structure, recommends an appropriate course of action, and moves quickly to restructure and implement change in the organization.

**Total Quality Management
(TQM)** A philosophy
of management that
concentrates on improving
the quality of a company's
products and services and
stresses that all operations
should head toward this
goal.

Two-Boss Employees
Employees who work on a
project-based team and are
responsible for coordinating
and communicating among
the functions and projects.

U

**Unemployment
Compensation** A policy
created by the Social
Security Act of 1935 to
protect workers who
lost their jobs due to
circumstances outside of
their own control.

V

Values Traits or
characteristics that
are considered to be
worthwhile and that
represent an individual's
priorities and driving
forces.

Index

N

nationality 84

National Labor Relations Act 242

newspapers 64

nonwage benefits 180

O

offer 106

open door policy 143

organizational chart 46

orientation 17, 111, 113, 124

OSHA 221, 227

overtime 38

P

part-time 63

pay grades 179

payroll 21, 221

payroll budget 17

peer review 151

performance appraisals 39

performance expectations 52

performance incentives 181

performance problems 251

performance standards 147

personal calls 118

personal conduct 38

personal days 206

personnel handbook 123

personnel policy 29

personnel records 39

pre-employment tests 160

pregnancy 206

prior employment 102

privacy 215

probationary 34

problem resolution 39

productivity 121, 197, 235

profit-sharing 212

promises 34

promotion 56

psychological tests 99

Q

quality-control programs 21

questions 84, 87

R

race 164

About the Author

After 30 years in the corporate world of Finance and Human Resource Management, Mary Holihan decided to strike out on her own. Combining a love of languages, reading, and writing with experience in the business world led to a new career as a freelance writer/editor/translator specializing in business subjects. Keeping one foot in the business world through research and contacts while having the freedom of the freelance world has turned out to be an ideal career.